Fearless Living
Yoga and Faith

Also by Swami Rama

BOOKS
Living with the Himalayan Masters
The Art of Joyful Living
Love Whispers
Meditation and Its Practice
The Royal Path: Practical Lessons on Yoga
Happiness Is Your Creation
Love and Family Life
A Practical Guide to Holistic Health
Path of Fire and Light, Vols. I and II
Spirituality: Transformation Within & Without
The Valmiki Ramayana Retold in Verse, Vols. I and II
Book of Wisdom: Ishopanishad
Celestial Song/Gobind Geet
Choosing a Path
Freedom from the Bondage of Karma
Perennial Psychology of the Bhagavad Gita
Wisdom of the Ancient Sages: Mundaka Upanishad
Japji: Meditation in Sikhism
Nitnem: Spiritual Practices of Sikhism
Philosophy/Faith of Sikhism
Sikh Gurus—Lives and Teachings

CO-AUTHORED BY SWAMI RAMA
Joints and Glands Exercises
Meditation and Christianity
Science of Breath
Yoga and Psychotherapy

AUDIO & VIDEO
Guided Meditation for Beginners
A Guide to Intermediate Meditation
A First Step Toward Advanced Meditation
Guided Meditation for Initiates
Inner Peace in a Troubled World
Stressless Living
Spiritual Origins of Health
Finding Meaning in Life
How to Tread the Path of Superconscious Meditation

Fearless Living
Yoga and Faith

by

Swami Rama of the Himalayas
Edited by Linda Johnsen

HIMALAYAN INSTITUTE®
PRESS
HONESDALE, PENNSYLVANIA, USA

The Himalayan Institute Press
952 Bethany Turnpike
Honesdale, PA 18431

www.HimalayanInstitute.org

©2005 The Himalayan International Institute of Yoga Science and Philosophy of the U.S.A.®
09   08   07   06   05
6   5   4   3   2   1

Printed in China

Cover design by Jeanette Robertson

The paper used in this publication meets the minimum requirements of American National Standard for Information Sciences—Permanence of Paper for Printed Library Materials, ANSI Z39.48-1984.

Library of Congress Cataloging-in-Publication Data

Rama, Swami, 1925–1996
  Fearless living : yoga and faith / [by Swami Rama] ; edited by Linda Johnsen.
      p. cm.
ISBN-13: 978-0-89389-251-7
ISBN-10: 0-89389-251-3
1. Spiritual life—Hinduism—Anecdotes. 2. Spiritual biography—India.
I. Johnsen, Linda, 1954– II. Title.
BL1237.32.R265 2005
294.5'436—dc22

2005022274

Contents

introduction

$\mathcal{S}$wami Rama's entire life was an adventure in faith. He left India with only $6 in his pocket when his guru, India's legendary Bengali Baba, sent him to the West to introduce the world to the immense benefits of yoga. Within just a few years, his work at the Menninger Foundation in Topeka, Kansas, radically transformed our ideas about how the mind affects the body, while his books and lectures on yogic diet and exercise helped spark the Holistic Health movement. Today many of the stress-reduction techniques he pioneered are routinely taught in hospitals across Europe and the Americas, and foods he helped introduce (such as basmati rice) are staples in Western health-food stores. Meditation classes are now offered from coast to coast, since dozens of scientific studies have verified the astonishing therapeutic effect of simply sitting quietly, focusing on a mantra.

Where did this remarkable man come from? Swami Rama was born in northern India in 1925, but lost both parents at an early age. He was adopted by the yogi-saint people called Bengali Baba, a living legend in India. Raised in the cave monasteries of the Himalayan mountains, Swamiji was initiated in advanced techniques of yoga and meditation. (Years later in a lab in Topeka, he would demonstrate his complete mastery of his physiological and mental states, amazing researchers who till that time had not believed such total control of internal states was humanly possible.) In his early twenties Swamiji was named Shankaracharya of Karvirpitham, one of the most prestigious spiritual posts in all of India. He was destined, however, to teach not just in India but throughout the world. He renounced his position and returned to his spiritual master for further training in the ancient techniques of yoga. In the late 1960s Bengali Baba sent this head-strong yogi to the West not merely to teach but also to personally demonstrate how spiritual practice can unveil higher, hidden dimensions in our nature.

For those of us who studied with Swami Rama, the best times were when he'd sit back and tell us about his experiences as a wandering ascetic in India, hiking in the Himalayan foothills or camping along the bank of the Narmada River. The tales of the saints and sages he'd met were so incredible we could hardly believe them, having been so conditioned by our scientific culture to turn our backs on the miraculous. He pointed us toward a truth beyond belief, a higher science that any one of us could verify for ourselves, as he had done. We needed only to diligently practice the techniques for expanding the boundaries of human awareness developed by spiritual masters thousands of years ago, and reverently handed down from guru to disciple over the millennia. Swamiji's own phenomenal abilities, called *siddhis* or supernatural powers, convinced us that his tales were true. These, he insisted, were trite gifts of the ancient tradition. The real value of our practice was health, tranquility, and enlightened awareness. If we supplemented our burgeoning faith with spiritual disciplines, we would no longer simply believe in a higher reality, we would experience it directly.

l e a r n i n g   t o   t r u s t

𝒻or so many of us today, trusting in a higher power isn't easy. We read about miracles that happened many years ago, when Jesus was teaching in Palestine, for example. But today most of the miracles we hear about are produced by science: miraculous new cures, new technologies, new breakthroughs. And scientists seem united in insisting there is no higher power, no ultimate meaning in life, nothing but the random reshuffling of DNA, atoms, and the void.

Can this really be true?

Not if the world Swami Rama invites us to enter is genuine. In the universe of yoga, consciousness, not matter, is the fundamental matrix. Spiritual maturity, not survival of the fittest, is the purpose of our existence. And from higher dimensions our senses can't penetrate emanate waves of grace to guide and protect us on our way. Most of us know intuitively that Swami Rama's world is the real one. But it helps to hear his true stories from a culture where the doors to the higher dimensions have not been closed and faith is not blind because it's based on actual experience.

Our faith is not misplaced if we turn to the elder brothers and sisters of our race, the great sages, who taught us how to live healthfully, ethically, and joyfully in the unlimited, interconnected field of higher awareness. Swami Rama grew up in the Himalayas, where the living reality of this field is still a part of daily reality. When he came to the West, he brought this knowledge with him and awakened us to the divine presence right here in our own homes and cities, which we had unconsciously been ignoring. He taught us to trust our deepest instincts, the ones that tell us that all of life really is mraculous, and every experience is pregnant with meaning.

The stories here are collected from Swami Rama's previous books and lectures. In "Humble, Happy, and Wise," Swami Rama explains how the sages helped shift him from an ego-centered orientation—not unlike our own—to richer understanding. In "Faith and Fearlessness," he shows how they gently pushed him beyond his fears, transforming him into the intrepid world teacher we were fortunate to know. The next four chapters reveal him exploring the world of spirit, watching a higher power at work leading, healing, saving, and enlightening those who surrender to its grace.

In the final chapter Swami Rama ends his reminiscing and begins to teach—for the purpose of his stories is never merely to entertain us, but to inspire us to take up spiritual life ourselves, to begin the practice of yoga and meditation, and to actively enter the universe of spirit ourselves. When we embark on this journey, the need for faith eventually falls away, replaced by our own direct experience of inner light.

This book is a small sampling of Swami Rama's many anecdotes, true stories of faith, protection, and revelation as he actually lived them. Seeing with the eye of faith, based on direct personal experience, Swamiji became an ambassador for the great souls who still hide themselves away in Himalayan caves and forests, and yet irradiate the entire world with their luminous blessing power. These elders of our race invite us to learn to fly without wings, to trust in a higher power, a divine purpose, and the ceaseless flow of grace that pours from the very heart of the universe. I hope Swamiji's experiences will enliven your faith and inspire you to set out on your own equally amazing spiritual adventure.

—Linda Johnsen

chapter one

Humble, Happy, and Wise

Swami Rama was not an ethereal figure floating over the earth on a cloud of light. He was more like a thunderstorm, dynamic and boisterous. He was a huge man, well over six feet tall, with an electric presence that could knock you off your feet if you weren't adept at keeping your balance. He had a huge ego, though paradoxically he wasn't egotistical at all. "Your ego should be like a comfortable old shoe," he would say. "You should be able to slip it on when you need it, but you should also be able to slip if off when you don't."

Swamiji often laughed about how his spiritual master, Bengali Baba, tried to teach him humility, the first step on the spiritual path. (You can't learn anything new if you think you already have all the answers!) Some of these lessons were funny, others were bitter and hard won. They were rooted in the principle that spiritual life begins with sacrifice. For orthodox Hindus in India, that might mean sacrificing flowers, fruit, grains, and oil into a ritual fire. But for yogis it means sacrificing the "little self" of our *work-a-day consciousness into the fire of knowledge so that the "Big Self" of higher awareness can begin to shine through.*

It's important to have faith in ourselves. But it's even more important to have faith in the Greater Self lying at the base of our being. For that to occur, the ego rooted in an inflated sense of self-importance has to go. Here are some of the stories Swamiji told about the "attitude adjustments" administered by his mentors that helped put him on track to spiritual life.

EGO AND VANITY ARE IN VAIN

*O*nce my master lived in a holy place of the Himalayas called Tungnath. On the way to see him I stopped at Karnaprayag, a shrine in the mountains. A renowned swami, Prabhat Swami, lived in a cave near the shrine, so I went to visit him. He was seated on a blanket, which had been folded into quarters, and a few villagers were seated before him. I greeted him according to our tradition. I expected him to offer me a seat beside him. I was being trained to be a swami at that time, and I was still suffering from an inflated ego, at least partly because people in the villages of India respect all swamis and bow down to them. This feeds the ego and creates many problems for a swami in training.

Prabhat Swami knew my problem. He smiled and said, "Please take your seat."

I asked, "Could you please unfold your blanket so I can sit next to you?" I insisted, but he just laughed at me. I asked, "Why won't you let me sit next to you?" I was quite conceited and impolite.

He quoted the dialogue between Rama and Hanuman in the *Yoga Vasishtha* [an Indian classic describing the universe from a yogi's point of view] saying, "'Eternally we are one and the same, but as human beings, you are still a servant and I am your master.' Modern man tries to have the position of a master without attaining anything."

Then he gave me a lesson, saying, "A man went to see a master who was seated on a high platform teaching many people. The man held a distinguished position in society, so he chafed at being treated like all the rest of the students, without getting special attention. He went up to the master and asked, 'Sir, can I sit on the same platform with you?'

"The master said, 'You should know the role of a student as well as the role of a master.'

"The man asked, 'Sir, what are the duties of a student?'

"The master explained, 'A student cleans, serves, washes dishes, cooks food, prepares and purifies himself, and serves his master.'

"Then the man asked, 'And what does a master do, sir?'

"'A master teaches—he doesn't do any of the menial work.'

"'Why can't I become a master without doing all of this?' asked the man. 'The menial work has nothing to do with my learning how to teach.'

"The master said, 'No, you will be hurting yourself and hurting others. You have to understand from the very beginning that the spiritual path can tolerate everything but ego.'"

Ego places a veil between the aspirant and the process of learning. When you become egocentric, you isolate yourself and are not able to communicate with your teacher or with your own conscience, and you don't follow the instructions of the teacher. Such an ego needs austerities and modifications, without which all knowledge drains away.

My Swollen Ego

*D*uring the rainy season swamis do not travel but stay in one place for four months. People come to learn the scriptures from them. Although I was still being trained as a swami, I too would teach every day. Students often create problems for a teacher. For instance, the first thing they do is place him high above them so that there is limited communication. My students built a high platform on which I was asked to sit. I was inordinately proud that I had a large following. That happens when you are a neophyte and hanker after name and fame. The more one's followers increase, the more egotistical one becomes.

I had the impression that one particular swami among my students was not very knowledgeable. During my lectures he sat quietly in a corner. This swami was actually an advanced adept, although I was not aware of it. He had come because I prayed to the Lord, "Lord, enlighten me. Help me, Lord." I sincerely cried and prayed, so the Lord sent that man to me. And what did I do? I gave him my loincloth to wash, and all day I would order him to do things for me. He was with me for two months before he decided to teach me a lesson.

One morning we were both sitting on a rock on a bank of the Ganga [Ganges River]. While brushing my teeth, I ordered, "Go and fetch me some water." He had had enough of my swollen ego. He said, "Go on brushing." I lost awareness of what was happening after that. Two days later someone found me lying there. My face was horribly swollen. I had dropped the brush but was still continuously rubbing my finger in my mouth. I was doing it unconsciously.

My master appeared and said, "Get up!" I opened my eyes but could not lift my face, it was so heavy. My gums were swollen and I could not move my jaw. Then my master told me, "That swami is a great sage. God sent him to you. You do not know how to be humble and behave properly with the men of God. Now I hope you have learned a lesson. Do not commit this mistake again." Then he said, "Get up; look at the sky and start walking."

I protested, "If I look at the sky and continue walking, I will stumble and fall."

He said, "Bow your head and then you will be able to walk without stumbling. For going through this hazardous journey of life, you must learn to be humble. Ego and pride are two stumbling blocks on this journey. If you are not humble, you cannot learn. Your growth will be stunted."

When one begins to tread the path of spirituality, it is essential to be humble. Ego creates barriers, and the faculty of discrimination is lost. If discrimination is not sharpened, reason does not function properly and there is no clarity of mind. A clouded mind is not a good instrument on the path of enlightenment.

INTUITION AND HUMBLENESS

*W*hen I was in Shrinagar, Kashmir, I met a great scholar of Vedanta [an influential school of philosophy in India, based on holy texts called the Upanishads] who was head of the department of philosophy in a renowned university. He said, "If I can answer your questions, I will be glad to do so."

So I put these questions to him: "The Upanishads appear to be full of contradictions. In one place they say that Brahman [the Supreme Reality, God as pure transcendence] is one without a second. Somewhere else they say that everything is Brahman. In a third place they say this world is false and Brahman alone is truth. And in a fourth place it is said that there is only one absolute Reality beneath all these diversities. How can one make sense out of these conflicting statements?"

He replied, "I don't know how to answer a swami's questions. You are learning to be a swami of the Shankaracharya order. You should know the answers better than I."

I went to many other learned people, but nobody could satisfy me. They could give me commentaries on different Upanishads, but no one could resolve these apparent contradictions. Eventually I went to a swami near Uttarkashi, 135 miles deep in the Himalayas. His name was Vishnu Maharaj. He was always naked, having no clothes or any other possessions. I said to him, "I want to know something about the Upanishads."

He said, "Bow down first. You are asking about the Upanishads with a swollen ego. How can you possibly learn these subtle truths?"

I did not like to bow down before anyone, so I left his place. After that, whenever I inquired about the Upanishads I was told, "Go to Vishnu Maharaj. No one else can answer you." But I didn't want to ask him because he knew that my whole problem was my ego, and he immediately tested me by saying, "Bow down and then I will answer your question." I wouldn't do that. I tried my best to find other swamis who could answer these questions, but everyone I asked referred me to Vishnu Maharaj.

Every day I would approach the cave where he lived on a bank of the Ganga. I would think, "Let me see how he answers my questions." But when I got near I would become very fearful of the impending confrontation, so I would change my mind and go back.

One day he saw me nearby and said, "Come, sit down. Are you hungry? Do you want to eat with me?" He was very pleasant and gracious. He gave me food and drink and then said, "Now you should go. I have no more time to spend with you today."

I said, "I have come with certain questions, sir. Food and drink I can get elsewhere. I want spiritual food."

He said, "You are not prepared. In your mind you want to examine me; you want to know whether I can reply to your questions or not; you don't want to learn. When you are prepared, come to me and I will answer you."

The next day I became very humble and I said, "Sir, the whole night I prepared myself, and now I'm ready!"

Then he taught me, and all my questions were resolved. Answering my questions systematically, he said that there are no contradictions in the teachings of the Upanishads. These teachings are received directly by the great sages in a deep state of contemplation and meditation. He explained, "When the student starts practicing, he realizes that this apparent world is changeable, while truth never changes. Then he knows that the world of forms and names, which is full of changes, is false, and that behind it there exists an absolute Reality that is unchanging. In the second step, when he has known the truth, he understands that there is only one truth and that truth is omnipresent, so there is really nothing like falsehood. In that stage he knows that reality that is one and the same in both the finite and infinite worlds. But there is another, higher, state in which the aspirant realizes that there is only one absolute Reality without second, and that that which is apparently false is in reality a manifestation of the absolute One.

"These apparent contradictions confuse only that student who has not studied the Upanishads from a competent teacher. A competent teacher makes the student aware of the experiences one has on various levels. These are the levels of consciousness, and there is no contradiction in them." He continued: "The teachings of the Upanishads are not understood by the ordinary mind or even by the intellectual mind. Intuitive knowledge alone leads to understanding them."

In fact I wanted to strengthen the knowledge I had received from my master, and knowingly posed such questions to others. The sages never answer questions posed without humbleness. The questions are resolved by humility itself. This great man taught me to rise above intellectual arguments and instructed me to allow intuition to flow uninterruptedly to answer such subtle questions.

LESSONS IN HUMILITY

As a young man I thought I had perfected myself and that I didn't need any further teaching or study. I felt there was no swami in India as advanced as I because I seemed to be more intellectually knowledgeable than others, and I was myself teaching many swamis. When I conveyed this inflated opinion of myself to my master, he looked at me and asked, "Are you drugged? What do you mean?"

I said, "No, really. This is the way I feel."

He returned to the subject a few days later. "You are still a child. You only know how to attend college. You have not mastered four things. Master them and then you will have attained something.

"Have a desire to meet and know God. But have no selfish desire to acquire things for yourself. Give up all anger, greed, and attachment. Practice meditation regularly. Only when you have done these four things will you become perfect."

Then he told me to visit certain sages. He said, "When you are with them you should be very humble. If you become obstinate or aggressive, you will be deprived of their knowledge. They will just close their eyes and sit in meditation." He said this because he knew that I was very obstinate and impatient.

He gave me a list of sages of different orders. They were his friends who had known me from a young age because I had been with him when he visited them. I had been quite mischievous. I used to pester them and throw things at them so that they would know I was around. Whenever they came to visit my master they would ask, "Is he still with you?"

First I went to see a swami who was renowned for silence. He had withdrawn from worldly concerns. No matter what happened around him, he never looked up. On my way I talked with villagers nearby. They told me, "He doesn't talk to anyone or look at anyone; he doesn't even eat. This is the third month he has been in the same place without getting up. We have never seen such a man." This state is called *ajagar-vritti*, which means "python's tendency." Just as a python remains in a dormant state for a long time, some sages do not move for many days but remain in a deep state of meditation.

When I found him he was lying on a hillock under a banyan tree, smiling, with his eyes closed, as though he were the lord of the universe. He never wore anything, whether it was summer, winter, or the rainy season. His skin appeared weatherproof, like that of an elephant. He did not own a thing, but he was utterly content.

When I first saw him lying that way, I thought, "At least he should have a little decency." Then I thought, "My master told me to visit him, and I know that my master would not waste my time. I am seeing only his body." I touched his feet. (According to custom, when we touch the feet of great men, they bless us.)

But he was not sensitive to external stimuli; he was somewhere else. Three or four times I said, "Hello, sir; how are you?" But he did not respond. There was no movement, no answer. Then I started massaging his feet. I thought he would be pleased, but he kicked me. That kick was so strong that I was thrown backward all the way down the hill, which was quite steep, and into a lake below. I fell against many trees and rocks on the way down and ended up with many painful bruises. I was vindictive. "What reason has he to do this? I came to him in reverence, massaged his feet—and he kicked me! He's not a sage. I'll teach him: I'll break both his legs! I'll give him double what he gave me!" I really wanted to retaliate. I decided that perhaps my master sent me to him to teach him a lesson.

When I returned to the hill to vent my anger, he was sitting up and smiling. He said, "How are you, son?" I said, "How am I? After kicking me and knocking me down the hill, you're asking how I am?"

He said, "Your master told you to master four things, and you have not even mastered one. I kicked you to test your control of anger. Now you are so angry that you cannot learn anything. You are not tranquil. You are still very immature. You don't follow the spiritual teaching of your master, who is so selfless. What could you possibly learn from me? You are not prepared for my teachings. Go away!"

Nobody had ever talked to me like that. When I thought about what he said, I realized that it was true; I was completely possessed by my anger.

He asked, "Do you know why we touch the feet of a sage?" Then he recited a beautiful Persian belief: "A sage gives the best part of his life, surrendering it at the lotus feet of the Lord. People ordinarily recognize you only by your face—but the face of the sage is not here; it is with his Lord. People find only feet here, so they bow to the feet."

He said, "You should have that humility when touching someone's feet. Now you cannot stay here. You will have to go."

I wept and thought, "A few days ago I thought I was perfect, but surely I am not." Then I said, "Sir, I will come back to you when I have really conquered my ego." And I departed.

All the kicks and blows of life teach us something. No matter whence they come, they are blessings in disguise if we learn their lesson. Buddha said, "For a wise man, there is nothing to be called bad. Any adversity of life provides a step for his growth, provided he knows how to utilize it."

I visited another swami and determined that no matter what he did, I would not get angry. He had a beautiful farm. He said, "I'll give you this farm. Would you like it?" I said, "Of course."

He smiled. "Your master told you not to be attached, and yet you are very quick to tie yourself to a farm." I felt very small. My mind seemed bent toward anger and attachment and not toward higher things.

Later I was sent to still another swami. He knew that I was coming. There was a small natural fountain on the way where we used to go and wash. He left some gold coins there. I stopped there and I found three of them. For a second I entertained the thought of picking them up. I did so, and tucked them inside my loincloth. Then I reconsidered: "But these coins are not mine. Why do I need them? This is not good." I put them back.

When I went to the swami, he was annoyed. I bowed before him and he said, "Why did you pick up the coins? Do you still have lust for gold? Get out. This is not the place for you."

I protested, "But I left them there."

He said, "You left them later on. The problem is that

you were attracted to them and picked them up in the first place."

From the experiences that these sages gave me, I began to realize the difference between book knowledge and experiential knowledge. I began to see my many weaknesses, and I did not find it pleasant. Finally I returned to my master. He asked, "What have you learned?"

"I have learned that I have intellectual knowledge, but I do not behave in accord with that knowledge."

He said, "This is the problem all intellectuals have. They become overly proud of their knowledge. Now I will teach you how to practice, so that you will know."

A human being may know enough, but that knowledge needs to be brought into daily life. If this is not done, the knowledge remains limited. We all know what to do and what not to do, but it is very difficult to learn how to be. Real knowledge is found not in knowing but rather in being.

PRACTICE MAKES PERFECT

Once when I was teaching about life and death, a swami quietly came in and sat with my students. I thought that he was a beginner, so I treated him as I treated the others. I was annoyed because he only smiled, while the others were conscientiously taking notes. I finally asked, "Are you listening to me?"

He said, "You are only talking, but I can demonstrate

mastery over life and death. Bring me an ant."

A large ant was brought. He cut it into three pieces and separated them. Then he closed his eyes and sat motionless. After a moment the three parts moved toward each other. They joined together, and the revived ant scurried away. I knew it was not hypnosis, or anything like that.

I felt very small before that swami. And I was embarrassed before my students because I only knew the scriptures without a firsthand understanding and mastery of life and death. I asked, "Where did you learn that?"

He said, "Your master taught me."

At that I became angry with my master and immediately went to him. Seeing me he asked, "What happened? Why are you once again allowing anger to control you? You are still a slave to your violent emotions."

I said, "You teach others things that you don't teach me. Why?"

He looked at me and said, "I have taught you many things—but you don't practice. That is not my fault! All these achievements depend on practice, not just on verbal knowledge of them. If you know all about the piano but don't practice, you will never create music. Knowing is useless without practice. Knowing is mere information. Practice gives direct experience, which alone is valid knowledge."

THE SAGE FROM
THE VALLEY OF FLOWERS

There was not much literature on the flowers and ecology of the Himalayas, but whatever was available, I tried my best to go through. After reading a book by a British author about the Valley of Flowers, a flame of burning desire arose in my heart. In the Himalayas there are countless varieties of lilies, rhododendrons, and other flowers, but I specifically was anxious to see one of two valleys.

I knew a sage who constantly traveled in the Valley of Flowers region of the Himalayas. He was very strong and healthy and about eighty years of age. He always carried a unique blanket. This blanket weighed approximately eighty to one hundred pounds. You might wonder how he made this blanket so heavy. Any piece of cloth he found during his travels, he would patch onto the blanket. It was a blanket of a thousand patches. He called it *gudari,* which means "blanket of patches," and people called him Gudari Baba.

In answer to my request to visit the Valley of Flowers he said, "If you would really like to see the Valley of Flowers and want to follow me, you will have to carry this blanket."

I agreed, but when I put the blanket on my shoulders, I stumbled under its weight. He asked, "How is it possible for a young man like you to be so weak when you are apparently so healthy?"

He picked up the blanket and said, "See how light it is?" Then he put it on my shoulders again. He knew my master and so he allowed me to follow him to the Valley of Flowers.

As I was following him this sage said, "No one can retain his memory when he goes through the Valley of Flowers during the blooming season. We should bring all the obstinate kids like you here and set them right. Those who try to be intellectual and argue with us should be brought here so that they understand their worth."

I said, "But I am following you."

He said, "Oh yes. You argue all the time and don't listen attentively. You are very proud of your intellectual knowledge. I do not know how to read and write. You are more educated than I. You have education, but I have control of mind."

I told him, "I also have control."

He replied, "We shall see."

I said, "Sir, first of all, please take away your blanket from my shoulders because it is difficult to carry."

He lamented, "Oh, the children of this modern age!"

He took his blanket from me and started conversing with it: "O my beloved blanket, nobody understands anything about you. No one knows that you are a living blanket."

I looked at him and thought, "This man is really crazy!"

The next morning a Japanese monk joined us. He was

equally anxious to see the Valley of Flowers. This Japanese monk also thought that Gudari Baba was a crazy man. He asked me, "Rama, can you explain why this man is carrying such a heavy load?" We started talking and I thought it would be nice to share these experiences with each other.

This monk was afraid of going to the Valley of Flowers all alone. Someone had told him that if any traveler goes to see this valley, he forgets everything and his senses do not coordinate in perceiving sense objects. The traveler loses his memory and smiles all the time. He said that this baba was the right person to guide us because he traveled in this region and knew all the trails.

The next day this Japanese monk started shivering with fever. He had lived in the jungles of Burma and had suffered from malaria. He had a temperature of 103 to 104 degrees and his pulse rate was very high. The baba said to him, "You told this boy that I was crazy. Do you want to see the living power of my blanket? Do you know that this blanket is not a mere blanket, but a living force? Do you want to get well? Then kneel down and be humble!" The baba covered the Japanese monk with the blanket.

The monk said, "I will be flattened! It's too heavy and I am a small man."

The baba said, "Keep quiet!" After a few minutes he took the blanket away from the monk. When he removed the blanket, it was shivering. The baba asked the monk, "What happened to your fever?"

He said, "Sir, I don't have a fever anymore."

The baba said, "This blanket is very generous and kind and has taken away your fever." The baba looked at me and said, "Do you want his fever to be cured forever?"

I said, "Yes, please."

The baba said, "But he calls me crazy. I don't think he deserves my help."

I said, "The sages are kind and great and they always forgive others."

The baba smiled and said, "Of course I will help him." We traveled together for fifteen days and the Japanese monk did not suffer from the fever again.

Nine miles outside of Badrinath on a side trail that leads to the Valley of Flowers, there is a small *guru dwara* (Sikh temple). We took our meal there. We rested that whole day in the temple and started our journey to the Valley of Flowers the next day.

The flowers were in full bloom as far as the eye could see. For the first few hours it was soothing to the senses and stimulating to the mind. But slowly I started noticing that my memory was slipping away. After five or six hours the baba asked, "Hey, you! Can you tell me your name?"

We were both so disoriented that we could not remember our names. We had completely forgotten them. I was only aware of my existence and had a hazy idea that I was with two other people. That's all. The fragrance of those flowers was so strong that we could not think rationally. Our ability to reason wouldn't function. Our senses were anesthetized. We had a faint idea of our existence and that of the things around us. Our talk to each other did not make any sense. We lived in this valley for a week. It was highly enjoyable. The baba made fun of us all the time and said, "Your education and strength have no value."

After we came out of the Valley of Flowers, the baba said, "Your joy was because of the influence of the fragrance of the flowers. You were not meditating. That's what marijuana and hashish do to people, and they think that they are in meditation. Look at me. I was not affected or influenced by the fragrance of those wildflowers. Ha, ha, ha! You have gone to college and have read many books. You have lived on the opinions of others so far. Today you had a good chance to understand and compare direct knowledge and the so-called knowledge that is really imitation. So far the opinions that you have are actually the opinions of others. Those who live on the opinions of others do not ever have the ability to decide and express their own opinions. Boys, this informative knowledge is not considered by us to be real knowledge. Even if you understand that direct knowledge alone is valid, you don't have control over the mind. The education given to modern children is very superficial. Without any discipline, control over the mind is not possible—and without control of the mind, direct experience is impossible."

The Japanese monk left for Bodh Gaya, and I lived with the baba for another fifteen days. He is a free wanderer of this region, and all the pilgrims have heard about him.

Spiritual Dignity Is Also Vanity

*A*fter I had renewed my resolve to follow the path of renunciation, my master thought I was feeling guilty, so he told me to live on a bank of the Narmada River, which flows through central India, and to practice certain austerities there. He instructed me to go to an isolated, dense forest thirty miles south of Kherighat, near Omkareshwar. The river there was full of crocodiles, and in the mornings and evenings several of them would lie on the sand along the river. I lived on the riverbank for six months without anyone disturbing me. I had only a water pot, a blanket, and two loincloths. People from a village six miles distant supplied me with milk and whole-wheat bread once a day. Those six months of intense physical and mental austerities were a high period in my life.

One day a party of big-game hunters came by and saw me sitting in meditation on the sand in the midst of many crocodiles, some of whom were lying just a few yards away from me. The hunters took my photograph without my noticing and sent it to a newspaper. Soon stories about me appeared in many newspapers. At that time the Shankaracharya of Karvirpitham, Dr. Kurtkoti, a highly intellectual man and a Sanskrit scholar of high repute, was searching for his successor. Shankaracharyas are considered to be the spiritual heads of India and occupy positions analogous to that of the pope in the Christian tradition. Dr. Kurtkoti instructed a few pandits to observe my daily routine from a distance. They stayed in the village at night and watched my activities during the day. They also collected information from others about my life.

After observing me for some time and carefully investigating my background, they approached me and tried to persuade me to consider becoming Shankaracharya. I was taken to Dr. Kurtkoti, and he took a liking to me. Then I went to my master and received his permission to accept the position. After a ceremony lasting eighteen days, I was installed as a successor of Jagat Guru Shankaracharya. [*Jagat Guru* means "world teacher." Shankaracharya was a yogi and sage who founded the ten orders of swamis in India.] I received thousands of telegrams from well-wishers all over the world, including messages from the pope and other spiritual heads. It was a strange experience for me—such a startling contrast to my six months of solitude and silence. I was less than thirty years old and they gave me such a great responsibility.

Dr. Kurtkoti believed in socioreligious reformation and handed over his files of valuable correspondence with other spiritual and political leaders. I had numerous meetings with various groups and leaders. I had a busy schedule of traveling and lecturing, and when I wasn't so engaged, people would come to see me from morning to evening and ask for my blessings. It became very difficult for me; I had no freedom. I thought, "I don't get any time to meditate and do my practices; I spend my whole day blessing people. This is not good."

I was not at all happy. My conscience said, "You are not meant for this. Leave!" So after two years I simply ran away, without any money in my pocket. One day I had a large mansion to live in and many cars, and the next I had nothing but the clothes I was wearing. Wanting to return to the Himalayas, I boarded the third-class section of a train that was headed where I wanted to go, even though I had no ticket. The people on the train must have wondered whose clothes I had stolen, because I was still wearing the costly garb of Shankaracharya. When the conductor came he forced me to get off at the next station because I had no money, and I didn't want to reveal my identity. I had never before committed such a crime as traveling without a ticket. I just bowed my head and got down, saying humbly, "Thank you for not prosecuting me."

The admirers and followers of Shankaracharya did not at all appreciate my resigning the dignity and prestige of the position. They felt that I was forsaking my responsibilities—but I had not been happy, and I never returned to that place again.

When I came to my master he said, "You have seen how worldly temptations follow a swami; how the world wants to absorb a spiritual person. Now nothing will affect you, because you have experienced positions, institutions, and renunciation. People expect a lot from their spiritual leaders. Do what you can to uplift and enlighten the people—but never forget your path."

chapter two

Faith and Fearlessness

*Nature gave us a highly effective warning system to keep
us out of trouble. It's called fear. It keeps us from sticking our
fingers in electrical sockets or tobogganing down cliff faces.
It can also prevent us from living our lives courageously or
trusting our intuition. When fear becomes paralyzing, it no
longer serves its original purpose of preserving our health
and well-being. Now it's the enemy that stops us from
achieving our full potential.*

*Spiritual life doesn't require us to do things that are stu-
pid, but it does force us to face our fears and expand
beyond self-imposed limitations. So often the source of our
fear is not some external event but our internal feelings
about it. Swami Rama's teachers in the Himalayas taught
him to see through the illusion of anxiety-provoking situations and have faith in a positive and enriching outcome.
This valuable lesson wasn't delivered only through words,
however. Swamiji's biggest breakthroughs occurred when
his mentors helped him directly confront his feelings.
Through trial and experiment, Swami Rama negotiated
the path of faith to the goal of fearlessness.*

FEAR OF SNAKES

*L*et me tell you about my fear. In my young age I was usually fearless. I could cross the swollen Ganga River and go into the forest without the slightest fear of tigers—but I was always very much afraid of snakes. I have had many encounters with snakes, but I concealed my fear from everyone, even my master.

Once, in September of 1939, my master and I came down to Rishikesh. We were on the way to Virbhadra, and camped at a spot where my ashram stands today. Early in the morning we took our bath in the Ganga and sat down on its bank for meditation. By that time I had already formed the habit of sitting for two or three hours without a break. It was about seven thirty when I opened my eyes—and saw that I was face to face with a cobra. The lower half of its body was coiled on the ground, and the upper half was raised. It was sitting very still, about two feet in front of me, looking at me. I was terrified and immediately closed my eyes again. I did not know what to do. After a few seconds, when I opened my eyes again and found that the snake had not moved, I jumped up quickly and ran away. After running for a few yards, I looked back and saw that the cobra was just starting to crawl back toward the bushes.

I went back to my master and explained what had happened. He smiled and told me that it is natural for any living creature to be in a state of meditation near someone who is in deep meditation.

Another time, after experiencing many kinds of training, I had another frightening experience with snakes. One cold rainy evening I went to a temple to ask for shelter. At first they said, "If you are a swami, why do you need shelter?" But then a lady came from the temple and said, "Come with me. I will give you shelter."

The woman took me inside a small, six-foot-square thatched hut and told me to stay there. Then she left. I had only a deerskin on which to sit, a shawl, and a loincloth. There was no light in the hut, but I could dimly see from the light that came through the entrance. After a few minutes I saw a cobra crawling in front of me—and then another one at my side. Soon I was aware that there were several cobras in the room. I realized that I had come to a snake's temple! It was a very dangerous situation, and I was afraid. The woman wanted to test whether I was a genuine swami or not, and I was actually just learning to be a swami. People believe a swami is high above any ordinary human being. In India, swami means one who is all-powerful, a healer, a preacher, and much more. A swami is put in such a difficult situation that it would drive an ordinary person crazy. People do not realize that some swamis are still beginners on the path, that others have trodden the path a bit, and that only a few have attained the goal.

I was very much afraid, but I thought, "If I run away at night, where could I go? And if I do leave, that woman will never give alms to swamis in the future." I decided, "I will remain here. Even if I die, at least the principles of renunciation will not have been found wanting."

Then I thought, "That woman does not appear to be enlightened, and yet she can come into this hut. So why can't I remain here without being harmed?" Remembering my master's words, I said to myself, "If I sit still, what will the cobras do to me? I have nothing that they want." I sat there the whole night watching, and the only thing I lost was my meditation. I could only meditate on the cobras.

Despite these two experiences, however, my fear of snakes continued. As a young swami many people, even high government officials, came and bowed before me and I blessed them. But within me was an obsessive fear of snakes. I would teach the *Brahma Sutra* [a terse classic text on Brahma, the transcendent reality], the philosophy of fearlessness, to my students, but fear was there inside me. I tried my best to remove the fear by intellectualizing it, but the more I tried, the stronger the fear became. It became so strong that it started creating problems. With any sudden noise the thought of snakes would come into my mind. When I sat for meditation I would often open my eyes and look about. Wherever I went I would look for a snake. Finally I said to myself, "You must remove this fear even if you die in the process. It is not good for your growth. How can you lead people who love, respect, and depend on you? You have this fear and yet you are guiding people—you are a hypocrite."

I went to my master and I said, "Sir?" He said, "I know what you want. You are afraid of snakes."

"If you knew, why didn't you tell me how to get rid of that fear?" I asked. He said, "Why should I tell you? You should ask me. Why did you try to hide this fear from me?" I had never kept any secret from him, but somehow I did not tell him about this fear.

Then he took me to the forest and said, "We are observing silence starting tomorrow at dawn. At three thirty in the morning you will get up and collect leaves and wildflowers for a special worship that we will do."

The next morning I found a big heap of leaves. As I picked up the heap in the darkness, I realized that there was a cobra in it. It was in my hand, and there was no escape. I did not know what to do. I was so frightened that I was on the verge of collapsing. My hands were trembling. My master was there and he said, "Bring it to me."

I was shaking with fear. He said, "It will not bite you."

The unconscious fear welled up nevertheless. My mind said, "It is death that you are holding in your hand." I believed my master, but my fear was stronger than my belief.

He said, "Why do you not love the snake?"

"Love?" I cried, "How can you love something when you are under the influence of fear?" This is a familiar situation in the world: if you are afraid of a person, you cannot love him. You will be unconsciously afraid of him all the time. The cause of fear grows in the unconscious.

My master said, "Look, it's such a beautiful creature. It roams all over, but look how clean and neat it is. You do not remain clean; you have to take a bath every day. A snake is the cleanest creature in the world."

I said, "It is clean, but it is also dangerous."

He told me, "Man is more unclean and poisonous than a snake. He can kill and injure others. Each day he projects poison in the form of anger and other negative emotions on those with whom he lives. A snake never does that. A snake bites only in defense."

He went on: "When you are fast asleep, does your finger prick your own eyes? Do your teeth bite your tongue? There is an understanding that all your limbs belong to one body. The day we have a like understanding that all creatures are one, we will not fear any creature."

I continued to hold the snake as he talked, and gradually my fear subsided. I began to think, "If I don't kill snakes, why should a snake kill me? Snakes don't bite anyone without reason. Why should they bite me? I am nobody in particular." My mind gradually began to function normally. Since that experience, I have not again been afraid of snakes.

Animals are instinctively very sensitive and are receptive to both hatred and love. If one has no intention to harm animals, they become passive and friendly. Even wild animals would like to associate with human beings. In the valleys of the Himalayas, I observed that animals would come near the villages at night and return to the forest early in the morning. They seem to want to be near human beings, but are afraid of the human's violent nature. A human being, with all his selfishness, attachments, and hatred, loses touch with his essential nature and thus frightens the animals, who then attack in self-defense. If a person learns to behave gently with animals, they will not attack him. I often remember the way Valmiki, [one of India's greatest poets], St. Francis, and Buddha loved animals, and I try to follow their example.

Fear gives birth to insecurity, which creates imbalance in the mind, and this influences one's behavior. If you examine a fear, you will usually find it is based on imagination, but that imagination can create a kind of reality. It is true that fear creates danger, and human beings then must protect themselves from that self-created danger. All of our dreams materialize sooner or later. Thus it is really fear that invites danger, though we usually think that danger brings on the fear. Fear is the greatest sickness that arises from our imagination. I have seen that all fears and confusion can easily be overcome with practical experience.

The first ten commitments of the *Yoga Sutra* [classic manual on yoga practice by the sage Patanjali] are prerequisites for attaining *samadhi* (the deepest states of meditation)—and the first is *ahimsa*. Ahimsa means non-killing, non-harming, and non-injury. By becoming selfish and egotistical, human beings become insensitive and lose the power of instinct. Properly used, instinct can help you on the path of ahimsa.

In all my years of roaming in the mountains and forests of India, I have never heard that any wild animal ever attacked a *sadhu* [wandering ascetic], swami, or yogi. These people do not protect themselves from the animals or natural calamities like avalanches. It is inner strength that makes one fearless, and it is the fearless one who transcends individual consciousness and becomes one with the universal consciousness. Who can kill whom? For Atman [the innermost soul] is eternal, though the body must return to dust sooner or later. This strong faith is enjoyed by all the sages in the lap of the Himalayas.

IN A TIGER'S CAVE

*O*nce I was traveling all alone in Tarai Bhavar toward the mountains in Nepal. I was on my way to Katmandu, which is the capital of Nepal. I walked twenty to thirty miles each day. After sunset I would build a fire, meditate, and then rest. I would begin walking again at four o'clock the next morning and walk until ten o'clock. Then I would sit near water under a tree through the middle part of the day, and travel again from three thirty until seven in the evening. I walked in my bare feet, carrying a blanket, a tiger skin, and a pot of water.

At about six o'clock one evening I became tired and decided to take a short nap in a cave, which was about two miles from the nearest road. I spread my blanket on the floor of the small cave because it was a little damp. As soon as I lay down and closed my eyes, I was pounced on by three little tiger cubs, who made gentle cries and pawed at my body. They were hungry and thought that I was their mother. They must have been only twelve to fifteen days old. For a few minutes I lay there petting them. When I sat up, their mother was standing at the entrance to the cave. First I feared that she would rush in and attack me, but then a strong feeling came from within, and I thought, "I have no intention to hurt these cubs. If she leaves the entrance of the cave, I will go out." I picked up my blanket and pot of water. The mother tiger backed off from the entrance and I went out. When I had gone about fifteen yards from the entrance, the mother tiger calmly went in to join her babies.

Such experiences help one to control fear and give a glimpse of the unity that lies between animals and human beings. Animals can easily smell violence and fear. Then they become ferociously defensive. But when animals become friendly, they can be very protective and help human beings. One human being may desert another in danger, but animals rarely do so. The sense of self-preservation is of course strong in all creatures, but animals are more dedicated lovers than human beings. Their friendship can be relied upon. It is unconditional, while relationships between people are full of conditions. We build walls around ourselves and lose touch with our own inner being and then with others. If the instinctive sensitivity for our relation to others is regained, we can become realized without much effort.

MISTAKEN FOR A GHOST

*W*hen I was staying in the Nanital forests in the Himalayan foothills, I would sometimes come down to a small city at the height of six thousand feet. People there would chase after me for blessings and advice, as they do with most yogis and swamis. In order to have time to do my practices, I found it necessary to protect myself from visitors. I heard about a British cemetery that was quiet and neatly kept. Wearing a long white gown made from a blanket to protect myself from the cold, I went to the cemetery to meditate at night.

One night two policemen who were patrolling that area walked through the cemetery, flashing lights here and there looking for vandals. I was sitting in meditation on the broad monument of a British military officer. My whole body, including my head, was covered with the blanket. The policemen flashed their lights in my direction from some distance away and were startled to see a humanlike figure covered with a blanket. They went to the police station and told the other officers that they had seen a ghost in the cemetery. This rumor spread all over the city and many people were frightened.

The superintendent of police came to the cemetery the next night with several armed policemen and flashed light on me once again. In that state of meditation I was not aware of them, so I did not stir. They all thought I was a ghost. They drew their revolvers to shoot at me because they wanted to see if bullets would affect a ghost. But the superintendent of police said, "Wait, let us challenge the ghost first. Perhaps it is not a ghost, but some person." They came closer and surrounded the monument on which I was sitting. But they still could not figure out what was inside the blanket. Then they fired a shot into the air. Somehow I became aware of them and came out of my meditation. I uncovered myself and asked, "Why are you disturbing me here? What is it you want of me?"

The superintendent of police, who was British, knew me very well. He apologized for disturbing me and ordered the policemen who patrolled that area to supply me with hot tea each night. Thus the mystery of the ghost was solved.

Mr. Peuce, the superintendent of police, then started visiting me regularly. He wanted to learn meditation from me. One day Mr. Peuce asked me about the nature of fear in man. I said that among all the fears, the fear of dying is deeply rooted in the human heart. The sense of self-preservation leads one to many hallucinations. A human being is constantly haunted by fears. He loses his balance and starts imagining and projecting his ideas the way he wishes. He deepens this process by repeating it again and again. Fear is the greatest enemy of man. Mr. Peuce was very much afraid of ghosts and wanted to know if I had ever seen one. I said, "I have seen the king of ghosts—and that is man. A man is a ghost as long as he identifies himself with the objects of his mind. The day he becomes aware of his essential nature, his true self, he is free from all fears."

It is of no use to live under the pressure of fear, for there is no joy in being afraid in every step of life. Without encountering the fears, we only strengthen them. On the path of spirituality, fear and sloth are the prime enemies.

THE DEVIL IN THE DREAM

One evening after my brother disciple and I had walked thirty miles in the mountains, we stopped to rest two miles beyond Kedarnath. I was very tired and soon fell asleep, but my sleep was restless because of my extreme fatigue. It was cold and I did not have a blanket to wrap around me, so I put my hands around my neck to keep warm. I rarely dream. I had dreamt only three or four times in my life, and all of my dreams had come true. That night I dreamt that the devil was choking my throat with strong hands. I felt as though I were suffocating.

When my brother disciple saw my breath rhythm change and realized that I was experiencing considerable discomfort, he came to me and woke me up. I said, "Somebody was choking me!" Then he told me that my own hands were choking me.

That which you call the devil is part of you. The myth of the devil and of evil is imposed on us by our ignorance. The human mind is a great magician. It can assume the form of both a devil and a divine being any time it wishes. It can be a great enemy or a great friend, creating either hell or heaven for us. There are many tendencies hidden in the unconscious mind that must be uncovered, faced, and transcended on the path of enlightenment.

Dreaming is a natural state of mind. It is an intermediate state between waking and sleeping. When the senses are prevented from receiving sense perceptions, the mind starts recalling the memories from the unconscious. All the hidden desires also lie in the unconscious, waiting to find their fulfillment. When the senses are not perceiving the objects of the world and the conscious mind is at rest, then recalled memories start coming forward and they are called dreams. Through dreams we can analyze a level of our hidden personality. This analysis is sometimes helpful in curing certain ailments. With the help of meditation, we can consciously recall these memories, observe them, analyze them, and resolve them forever.

There are various types of dreams. In addition to the painful and pleasant dreams that we ordinarily experience, there are another two categories of dreams. One is a prophetic dream, and the other is a nightmare. Sometimes prophetic dreams are guiding. Nightmares are the signs of intense agony created by frustrations. They can also occur if someone is overly tired or has bad digestion.

I have never heard anyone claiming to have seen a devil in the daytime. My brother disciple, with the help of a simile, told me, "A rope in darkness can be mistaken for a snake. A mirage in the distance can be mistaken for water. Lack of light is the main cause of such a vision. Does the devil exist? If there is only one existence, which is omnipresent and omniscient, then where is the place for the existence of the devil? Those who are religiously sick believe in the existence of the devil by forgetting the existence of God. A negative mind is the greatest devil that resides within the human being. Transformation of negativity leads toward positive or angelic visions. It is the mind that creates hell and heaven. Fear of the devil is a phobia that needs to be eradicated from the human mind."

FROM FEAR TO FAITH

Students are many; disciples are few. Many students came to my master and requested, "Please accept me as your disciple." They all showed their faithfulness by serving him, by chanting, by studying, and by practicing. He did not respond. One day he called everyone to him. There were twenty students. He said, "Let's go." Everyone followed him to the bank of the Tungbhadra River in southern India. It was in full flood, wide and dangerous.

He said, "He who can cross this river is my disciple."

One student said, "Sir, you know I can do it, but I have to go back to finish my work." Another student said, "Sir, I don't know how to swim." I didn't say anything. As soon as he said it, I jumped. He sat down quietly as I crossed the river. It was very wide. There were many crocodiles, and huge logs were rolling with the currents of water, but I was not concerned. My mind was one-pointed on completing the challenge I was given. I loved to be challenged, and I always accepted a challenge joyfully. It was a source of inspiration for me to examine my own strength. Whenever I was tired I would float, and in this way I succeeded in crossing the river.

My master said to the other students, "He didn't say that he was my disciple, but he jumped."

I was close enough to him to know his power. I thought, "He wants his disciples to cross the river. Here I am. I can do it. It's nothing, because he is here. Why can't I do it?" So firm were my faith and determination.

Faith and determination, these two are the essential rungs on the ladder of enlightenment. Without them the word *enlightenment* can be written and spoken, but never realized. Without faith we can attain some degree of intellectual knowledge, but only with faith can we see into the most subtle chambers of our being. Determination is the power that sees us through all frustrations and obstacles. It helps in building willpower, which is the basis of success within and without. The scriptures say that with the help of *sankalpa shakti* (the power of determination) nothing is impossible. Behind all great work and all great leaders of the world stands this shakti. With this power behind him, such a leader says, "I will do it; I have to do it; I have the means to do it." When this power of determination is not interrupted, one inevitably attains the desired goal.

LOST IN THE LAND OF *DEVAS*

I had heard and read so much about a village called Jñanganj that my desire for visiting it became intense. Many pilgrims have heard about Jñanaganj, but it is rare that someone perseveres enough to reach there. This small community is situated deep within the lap of the Himalayas, on the border between Tibet and Pithora Garh. For eight months of the year one cannot enter or come out of it (due to severe weather), but a small community of yogis lives there year-round. These yogis observe silence and spend most of their time in meditation. Small log houses provide shelter, and their main food is potatoes and barley, which they store for the whole year. The community includes Indian, Tibetan, and Nepalese sadhus. There is no other place but this that can be called Jñanganj.

I decided to visit this village and Mount Kailas along with another four renunciates. We went from Almora to

Dorhchola to Garbiank, but after several days we lost our way. It was the month of July when the snow melts in the Himalayan mountains. We found glaciers collapsing, blocking the way behind and in front of us. I was accustomed to such sudden calamities, but the other swamis were new to these adventures, and they were very much frightened. They held me responsible because I was from the Himalayas. They said, "You should have known better. You are from the mountains. You misguided us. We have no food, the path is blocked, it is very cold. We are dying here."

We were stranded there by the side of an enormous lake called Rakshastal, which means "Lake of the Devil." Because of the melting snow and avalanches, the water started rising. By the second day everyone was in panic. I said, "We are not ordinary worldly people. We are renunciates. We should die happily. Remember God. Panic is not going to help us."

Everyone started remembering his mantra and praying, but nothing seemed to help. Their faith was tested— but none of them had any. They were afraid of being buried in the snow. I started joking and said, "Suppose you all die: what will be the fate of your institutions, wealth, and followers?"

They said, "We may be dying, but first we will see that you die." My jokes and taking the situation lightly made them more angry.

Few people know how to enjoy humor. Most people become very serious in such adverse situations. Humor is an important quality that makes one cheerful in all walks of life. When the poison was given to Socrates, he made a few jokes. When the cup of hemlock was given to him he said, "Can I share a bit of it with the gods?"

Then he smiled and said, "Poison has no power to kill a sage, for a sage lives in reality, and reality is eternal." He smiled and took the poison.

I said to these renunciates, "If we have to live and if we are on the right path, the Lord will protect us. Why should we worry?" It started becoming dark and again snow started falling. Suddenly a man with a long beard and a white robe and who was carrying a lantern appeared before us. He asked, "Have you lost your way?"

"For almost two days we have had nothing to eat, and we do not know how to get out of this place," we replied. He told us to follow him. There had seemed to be no way through that avalanche, but when we followed him, we eventually found ourselves on the other side. He showed us the way to a village, which was a few miles away, and instructed us to pass the night there. He then suddenly disappeared. We all wondered who he was. The villagers say that such experiences are not uncommon in this land of *devas* [angels]. These bright beings guide innocent travelers when they lose their way. We stayed in the village that night.

The next day the other four renunciates refused to travel with me. They all turned back. They did not want to go further into the mountains because they feared more dangers. After being given directions by the villagers I went alone toward Jñanganj. One of the sadhus there was kind enough to give me shelter, and I stayed for one and a half months. This place is surrounded by high snowy peaks and is one of the most beautiful places that I have ever seen.

Returning from Jñanganj, I came back by the way that leads to Manasarowar at the foot of Mount Kailas. I met many advanced Indian and Tibetan yogis. For a week I lived in a camp of lamas at the foot of Mount Kailas. I still treasure this experience. I traveled to Garviyauk with a herd of sheep. The shepherds with whom I traveled talked about the beings who guide travelers in the Himalayas. They narrated many such experiences to me. It is said that the devas are the beings who can travel between both the known and unknown sides of life. They can penetrate through physical existence to guide aspirants, and yet they live in the non-physical plane. The devas too have their plane of existence. Esoteric science and occultism talk much about such beings, but modern scientists dismiss this theory, saying that such beings are either fantasies or hallucinations.

Scientists have not yet studied many dimensions of life. They are still studying the brain and its various zones. The aspect of psychology that is termed transpersonal or transcendental psychology is beyond the grasp of modern science. The perennial psychology of the ancients, which has been cultivated for centuries, is an exact science. It is based on the finest knowledge—intuition. The physical sciences have limitations, and their investigations are only on the gross levels of matter, body, and brain.

chapter three

The Mysterious Mind

Mind over matter? Mind over mind? Could psychic powers possibly be real? Swami Rama told us, "The mind is a reservoir for numerous powers. By using the resources hidden within it, we can attain any height of success. If the mind is trained, made one-pointed and inward, it also has the power to penetrate into the deeper levels of our being. It is the finest instrument."

When he was in the mood, Swamiji used to show us his amazing psychic abilities. He read our minds as if they were newspapers, made flowers bloom out of season, even made gallons of tasty chai pour from a quart-size thermos. But after the first year or two in America, he stopped these displays almost entirely. "Now people are coming just to watch me do miracles, not to learn how to discipline their minds," he complained.

Fortunately for us, he continued telling stories about the masters whose powers he'd witnessed in the Himalayas. Some of those stories are presented for you here. He told these to jolt us out of the spiritual stupor born of our materialist worldview. He wanted us to understand that there is much more to this universe than our scientists here in the West have discovered so far. He wanted us to know that our minds have virtually unlimited potential, and that we must have faith in our extraordinary inner resources.

LESSONS ON THE SANDS

If you look at someone with full attention by focusing your conscious mind, you will immediately influence him. A swami taught me this when I was young. His name was Chakravarti. He was one of the most eminent mathematicians of India and the author of *Chakravarti's Mathematics.* Later he renounced the world to become a swami, and he was a student of my master. He contended that gazing *(trataka)* is a powerful tool for influencing the external world and for strengthening concentration.

When the mind is focused on an object, it is called trataka; when it is focused internally, it is called concentration. The power of a focused mind is immense. There are various methods of trataka, each of which gives a different power to the human mind. You may gaze at the space between the two eyebrows, the bridge between the two nostrils, candlelight in a dark room, the early morning sun, or the moon. But certain precautions must be observed to avoid both physical and mental injury.

The power of thought is known all over the world. A one-pointed mind can do wonders, but when we direct it toward worldly gains we are caught in the whirlpool of selfish desires. Many on the path fall victim to the temptations of acquiring *siddhis* [supernatural powers] and forget their real goal of attaining serenity, tranquility, and self-realization.

One day Chakravarti said to me, "Today I am going to

show you something. Go to the court and find a person who is being persecuted unjustly."

So I asked one of the lawyers, "Can you tell me of anyone who is being tried unjustly in this court?"

He said, "Yes, I have such a case."

I went back, and Swamiji said: "Okay, this man will be acquitted, and I will now tell you word for word the judgment that will be handed down." He dictated the judgment to me, although he was not a lawyer. He said, "I have made three mistakes purposefully. The judgment will be exactly like my dictation, and it will also have these three mistakes." I typed up his dictation.

When the judgment was later handed down, every word, comma, and period was exactly the same as what had been dictated to me. He said, "Compare my dictation with the judgment and you will find that the same two commas and one period are missing." The dictation perfectly matched the judgment.

I said, "Swamiji, you can change the course of the world."

He said, "I don't claim to do that; that is not my purpose. I am demonstrating this so that you can understand how a man can influence the mind of another from any part of the world if it is for a good reason. Helping others is possible from a distance."

I asked him to give me the secret of this power. He said, "I will give you the secret, but you won't want to practice it." I did practice the method for some time and it helped me, but later I discontinued it because it was distracting and time consuming.

Swami Chakravarti also taught me philosophy through mathematics. He explained every digit with verses from the Upanishads. From zero to one hundred, he explained the philosophical meaning of the science of mathematics. In mathematics all digits are multiples of the number one. Similarly, there is only one absolute reality, and all the names and forms of the universe are multiple manifestations of that One. Drawing lines on the sand of the Ganga with his staff, he made a triangle and taught me how life should be an equilateral triangle. The angle of the body, the angle of internal states, and the angle of the external world make up the equilateral triangle of life. As all numbers are the outcome of a point that cannot be measured, similarly this whole universe has come from an unmeasurable void. Life is like a wheel, which he compared with a circle or zero. This circle is an expansion of the point. He used another analogy: "There are two points, called death and birth, and life here is a line between the two. The unknown part of life is an infinite line."

My aversion to the study of mathematics was dispelled, and I began studying mathematics with considerable interest. I learned that mathematics is the basis of all sciences, but it is itself based on the exact science of Sankhya philosophy. Sankhya philosophy is the most ancient philosophy for knowing the body, its components, and various functions of the mind. By understanding Sankhya, all the philosophical questions arising in my mind were easily solved, and I understood the scriptures properly.

The last day of his teaching was enchanting. He said, "Now make a zero first, then put one afterwards: 01. Every zero has value if the one is put first, but zero has no value if the one is not put first. All the things of the world are like zeros, and without being conscious of the one reality, they have no value at all. When we remember the one reality, then life becomes worthwhile. Otherwise it is burdensome."

Then Swami Chakravarti left for the deep Himalayas and I never met him again. I am grateful to those teachers who spent their valuable time teaching me.

TRANSMUTATION OF MATTER

In 1942 I started on a journey to Badrinath, the famous Himalayan shrine. On the way there is a place called Shrinagar, which is situated on a bank of the Ganga. Five miles from Shrinagar there is a small shakti temple, and just two miles below that was the cave of an aghori baba. Aghora is a mysterious path that is rarely mentioned in the literature and hardly understood even by the yogis and swamis of India. It is an esoteric path involving solar science. It is used for healing. This science is devoted to understanding and mastering the finer forces of life—finer than *prana* [life energy]. It creates a bridge between life here and hereafter. There are very few yogis who practice the aghori science, and those who do are shunned by most people because of their strange ways.

The villagers in the area around Shrinagar were terrified of the aghori baba. They never went near him, because whenever anyone approached him, he called them names and threw pebbles at them. He was about seventy-five years old, over six feet tall, and strongly built. He had long hair and a beard and wore a jute loincloth. He had nothing in his cave except a few pieces of gunnysack.

I went to see him, thinking that I would pass the night there and learn something from him. I asked a local pandit to show me the way. The pandit said, "This aghori is no sage; he is dirty. You don't want to see him." But the pandit knew much about my master and me, and I persuaded him to take me to the baba's cave.

We arrived in the evening just before dark. We found the aghori sitting on a rock between the Ganga and his cave. He asked us to sit beside him. Then he confronted the pandit, saying, "Behind my back you call me names and yet you greet me with folded hands." The pandit wanted to leave, but the aghori said, "No! Go to the river and fetch me a pot of water." When the frightened pandit came back with the water, the aghori handed him a cleaver and said, "There is a dead body floating in the river. Pull it ashore, chop off the thigh and calf muscles, and bring a few pounds of the flesh to me." The aghori's demand shook the pandit. He became very nervous—and so did I. He was extremely frightened and did not want to carry out the aghori's wishes. But the aghori became fierce and shouted at him, saying, "Either you will bring the flesh from that dead body or I will chop you up and take your flesh. Which do you prefer?"

The poor pandit, out of deep anxiety and fear, went to the dead body and started cutting it up. He was so upset that he accidentally cut the first and second fingers of his left hand, and they started bleeding profusely. He brought the flesh to the baba. Neither the pandit nor I were then in our normal senses. When the pandit came near, the aghori touched the cuts on his fingers, and they were instantly healed. There was not even a scar.

The aghori ordered him to put the pieces of flesh into an earthen pot, to put the pot on the fire, and to cover the lid with a stone. He said, "Don't you know this young swami is hungry, and you also have to eat?"

We both said, "Sir, we are vegetarians."

The baba was irritated by this and said to me, "Do you think I eat meat? Do you agree with the people here that I am dirty? I too am a pure vegetarian."

After ten minutes he told the pandit to bring him the earthen pot. He gathered a few large leaves and said, "Spread these on the ground to serve the food on." The pandit did so with trembling hands.

Then the aghori went inside the cave to fetch three earthen bowls. While he was gone the pandit whispered to me, "I don't think I will live through this. This is against everything that I have learned and practiced all my life. I should commit suicide. What have you done to me? Why did you bring me here?"

I said, "Be quiet. We cannot escape, so let us at least see what happens."

The aghori ordered the pandit to serve the food. When the pandit took the lid off the pot and began filling my bowl, we were astonished to find a sweet called *rasgula,* which is made from cheese and sugar. This was my favorite dish, and I had been thinking of it as I was walking to the baba's cave. I thought it was all very strange. The aghori said, "This sweet has no meat in it."

I ate the sweet, and the pandit had to eat it too. It was delicious. The aghori gave the leftovers to the pandit to distribute among the villagers. He did this to prove that we had not been fooled by means of a hypnotic technique. All alone in the darkness the pandit left for his village, which was three miles from the cave. I chose to stay with the aghori to solve the mystery of how the food was transformed and to understand his bewildering way of living. "Why was the flesh of a dead body cooked, and how could it turn into sweets? Why does he live here all alone?" I wondered. I had heard about such people, but this was my first chance to meet one in person.

After I meditated for two hours we began talking about the scriptures. He was extraordinarily intelligent and well-read. His Sanskrit, however, was so terse and tough that each time he spoke it took a few minutes to decipher what he was saying before I could answer him. He was no doubt a very learned man, but his way was different from any other sadhu that I had ever met.

Aghora is a path that has been described in the *Atharva Veda* [a sacred Hindu scripture that deals with healing and spiritual science] but in none of the scriptures have I ever read that human flesh should be eaten. I asked him, "Why do you live like this, eating the flesh of dead bodies?"

He replied, "Why do you call it a 'dead body'? It's no longer human. It's just matter that is not being used. You're associating it with human beings. No one else will use that body, so I will. I'm a scientist doing experiments, trying to discover the underlying principles of matter and energy. I'm changing one form of matter to another form of matter. My teacher is Mother Nature; she makes many forms, and I am only following her law to change the forms. I did this for that pandit so that he would warn others to stay away. This is my thirteenth year at this cave, and no one has visited me. People are afraid of me because of my appearance. They think I am dirty and that I live on flesh and dead bodies. I throw pebbles, but I never hit anybody."

His external behavior was crude, but he told me that he was behaving that way knowingly so that no one would disturb him as he studied and so that he would not become dependent on the villagers for food and other necessities. He was not imbalanced, but to avoid people he behaved as though he were. His way of living was totally self-dependent, and although he continued to live in that cave for twenty-one years, no villager ever visited him.

We stayed up through the night and he instructed me, talking the entire time about his aghora path. This path was not for me, but I was curious to know about his life. He had the power to transform matter into different forms, like changing a rock into a sugar cube. The next morning he did many such things, one after another. He told me to touch the sand—and the grains of sand turned into almonds and cashews. I had heard of this science and knew its basic principles, but I had hardly believed such stories. I did not explore this field, but I am fully acquainted with the governing laws of the science.

At noon the aghori insisted that I eat something before leaving. This time he took out a different sweet from the same earthen jar. He was very gentle with me, all the time discussing the tantra scriptures. He said, "This science is dying. Learned people do not want to practice it, so there will be a time when this knowledge will be forgotten."

I asked, "What is the use of doing all this?"

He said, "What do you mean by 'use'? This is a science, and a scientist of this knowledge should use it for healing purposes and should tell other scientists that matter can be changed into energy and energy into matter. The law that governs matter and energy is one and the same. Beneath all names and forms there lies one unifying principle, which is still not known in its entirety by modern scientists. Vedanta and the ancient sciences described this underlying principle of life. There is only one life force, and all the forms and names in this universe are but varieties of that One. It is not difficult to understand the relationship between two forms of matter, because the source is one and the same. When water becomes solid, it is called ice; when it starts evaporating, it is called vapor. Young children do not know that these three are forms of the same matter, and that essentially there is no difference in their composition. The difference is only in the form it takes. The scientists today are like children. They do not realize the unity behind all matter, nor the principles for changing it from one form to another."

Intellectually I agreed with him, and yet I did not approve of his way of living. I said good-bye and promised to visit him again, but I never did. I was curious about the fate of the pandit who had gone to his village the previous night in a state of fear, so I went to see him. To my surprise he was completely changed and was thinking of following the aghori and becoming his disciple.

Where Is My Donkey?

When I stayed in Mau, a small city in Uttar Pradesh, I lived in a hut that was built for wandering swamis and sadhus. Most of the time I stayed in my room, doing my exercises and sitting in meditation. I came out for a short while in the morning and evening.

A laundryman washed clothes nearby. He had no wife or children—only a donkey. One day he lost his donkey.

He was so worried that he fell into a trance. People thought he was in samadhi.

In India people will do anything in the name of samadhi. They will even sell their homes and offer money to the person who has apparently attained that state. They believe that giving gifts is the way to express their love and devotion for a holy man. So when the laundryman sat in the same position for two days, people started placing money, flowers, and fruit around him. Two people declared themselves to be his disciples and began collecting money. But that laundryman did not stir. His followers encouraged others to come. They wanted everyone to know that they were the disciples of this great guru. Through word of mouth he soon became famous.

I heard from one of these "disciples" that there was a great man in samadhi, so I went to see him. There was indeed someone sitting very still with his eyes closed. Many people were sitting around him, chanting, "O Lord, bring him back. Hari Rama, Hari Rama, Hari Krishna, Hari Krishna."

I asked them, "What are you doing?"

They said, "He is our guru and he is in samadhi." I was curious and thought, "Let me see what happens when he comes out of this state."

After two days he opened his eyes. Everyone looked on expectantly to hear what profound sermon he would deliver—but when he came out of the trance he only said, "Where is my donkey?"

The desire with which one goes into meditation is a

prime factor. When a fool goes to sleep, he comes out as a fool. But if one meditates with the single desire for enlightenment, he emerges as a sage.

There is a fine distinction between the person who becomes preoccupied and pensive, and the aspirant who really meditates. Intense worry can drive the mind toward one-pointedness, but in a negative way. Through meditation the mind becomes positive, one-pointed, and inward. The outer signs and symptoms are similar. Worry makes the body inert and tense, but meditation makes it relaxed, steady, and still. For meditation, purification of the mind is essential; for worry it is not needed. When intense worry controls the mind, the mind becomes inert and insensitive. But if a great man contemplates on the miseries of the world, it is not a worry at all, but a loving and selfless concern for humanity. In this case the individual mind expands and unites itself with the cosmic mind. When the mind is engrossed one-pointedly in individual interests, it is called worry. When the mind is made aware of the misery of others, it starts contemplating positively. In both cases the mind can become one-pointed, but in the latter case consciousness is expanded.

When Saint John was put in the isolated cell on the island of Patmos, he worried because he thought that the message of his master would not reach the masses. But this sort of worry was not for the fulfillment of his own desires; it was the well-being of all that concerned him. Meditation is expansion, and worry is contraction.

The same power that can flow in negative grooves can also voluntarily be directed toward positive grooves. Therefore it is important for a student to purify the mind first and then to meditate. Without a disciplined and purified mind, meditation is not helpful on the path of enlightenment. Preparation is important. The preliminary steps—control of actions, speech, dietary habits, and other appetites—are essential requisites. Those who discipline themselves and then meditate receive valid experiences. They come in touch with their positive and powerful potentials. These experiences become guides in fathoming the deeper levels of consciousness. The untrained and impure mind cannot create anything worthwhile, but the meditative and contemplative mind is always creative. Both worry and meditation leave deep imprints on the unconscious mind. Worry creates several psychosomatic diseases, while meditation makes one aware of other dimensions of consciousness. If the aspirant knows how to meditate, he will naturally be free from his habit of worrying. Hatred and worry are two negative powers that control the mind. Meditation and contemplation expand the mind.

I concluded that the poor laundryman, though sitting still, was deeply engrossed in misery. He was in deep sorrow, and his mind lost its balance. In that state he became still without knowing where he was. In samadhi the mind is consciously led to higher dimensions of awareness. The aspirants who try to attain samadhi without purification of mind are disappointed, because an impure mind creates obstacles in attaining this state. Samadhi is the result of a conscious and controlled effort. It is a state of transcendent consciousness. Worry contracts the mind, while meditation expands it. Expansion of individual consciousness and union with the transcendent consciousness is called samadhi.

WHO WAS THAT OTHER GOPINATH?

I was staying on the other side of the Ganga, six miles from the city of Kanpur. I lived in a garden by the bank of the river. During those days I didn't care for anything of the world. I never went to the city, but many people wanted my attention. They would come with fruit and sit before me. To avoid being disturbed, I kept a stock of *malas* [rosaries with 108 beads] and when anyone came I would say, "First sit down and repeat this mantra two thousand times and then we will talk." Most of my visitors would leave the malas and quietly depart.

One afternoon the treasurer of the Reserve Bank of India at Kanpur, whose name was Gopinath, came to visit me with four people. They sat down and started chanting. They became so engrossed in chanting that the time slipped by unnoticed. At nine o'clock in the evening Gopinath suddenly opened his eyes and said, "Something terrible has happened!"

Everyone asked, "What is it?"

He said, "My niece was to be married at seven o'clock tonight. All the ornaments for the marriage ceremony are locked in my safe, and I have the only key with me here. Swamiji, what have you done to me?"

I replied, "I haven't done anything. The atmosphere here does that to you. It happens to everyone who comes here. You relax and forget the world's problems; you experience and enjoy divinity. Why are you so worried?"

"But the ornaments and jewelry that I have to give them are in my safe."

I said, "Look, did you really forget yourself in chanting today?"

He said, "That's why I am still here."

"Then don't worry. God will take care of the situation. If something bad can happen because of chanting the Lord's name, let it happen; something worse would happen without it."

They got into their horse cart and quickly returned to the city. When Gopinath arrived he anxiously asked what had happened. The people there were confused by his concern. They said, "What is the matter with you? The ceremony is over. Everything is fine."

He said, "I was on the other side of the Ganga and had my keys with me. What about the ornaments?"

They said, "You gave the ornaments. Have you lost your mind?"

His wife came and said, "You presented the ornaments ten minutes before the ceremony; now the marriage party is over and everyone is enjoying the food."

But the four people who were with him confirmed that he was with me, chanting. They said, "Either you are fools, or we are fools." They were quite disturbed because they could not reconcile the reports with their own memories. Gopinath completely lost his mental equilibrium.

He said, "I am Gopinath—but who was that Gopinath who came here?" When he went to the office the next day he wouldn't talk to anyone, except to ask one question. He would say, "I am only one Gopinath. Can you tell me who that was?" For three years he was obsessed. He had to resign from his job because of it.

His wife came to see me but I could not help. I asked, "Does he speak with you?"

She said, "Yes, but all the time he asks, 'Tell me, honey, who was that other Gopinath? Did he look exactly like me?'"

After this incident many people came running to me, saying, "You are a sage of great miracles."

I said, "You are praising me for nothing." Neither I nor they knew what had happened. And really, I did not know what happened.

Later I asked my master, "What was it?" My master said that it was possible that one of the sages from our tradition helped Gopinath because he was fully absorbed in chanting God's name.

Throughout my life it has been my personal experience that sages are kind and generous in guiding and protecting the devotees of God. As far as my experiences go, a sage can live in the Himalayas, yet can travel and project himself in any part of the world.

An Experience with a Psychic

On our way to Rishikesh in 1973 we stayed in one of the hotels in New Delhi. There I met Dr. Rudolph Ballentine, a psychiatrist and former professor at a medical school in the United States. He had recently toured through the Middle East and Pakistan. Dr. Ballentine told me about an experience he had at Connaught Place, which is a famous shopping center in New Delhi. A stranger had called him by name and then abruptly told him the name of his girlfriend in England.

The doctor asked, "How did you know these things?"

He said, "You were born on such and such date and your grandfather's name is such and such." Then the man told him something very personal, which no one except Dr. Ballentine knew. The doctor thought, "This is the person for whom I have come to India."

The man said, "Sir, give me five dollars," and the doctor obliged. The man was looking here and there because he was afraid the police might see him. If the police had known what he was doing, they would have arrested him. He said, "Stay here. I will come right back." The doctor waited for half an hour, but the man did not return.

Dr. Ballentine told me, "Swamiji, he was a great man."

I asked, "What did he do?"

He answered, "He told me all those personal things about myself although I was a complete stranger."

I replied, "Didn't you already know those things?"

"Yes."

"Then what big thing did he do? If somebody knows what you are thinking, then you obviously already know it too. This knowledge doesn't improve you in any way. This ability may amaze you for some time, but it cannot help anyone in self-growth."

Fakes like the one Dr. Ballentine encountered are often disguised as sadhus at Connaught Place, revealing the past and predicting the future. They learn such tricks just to make their living. Naive tourists mistake them for great sages. Such tourists never meet the real sages. These pretenders give a bad name to spirituality and to spiritual people.

Dr. Ballentine then started traveling with us. When we left India he stayed in Rishikesh and traveled to other parts of India for several months, visiting the schools of Indian medicine. He returned to the United States and joined the Himalayan Institute [an organization founded by Swami Rama for the promotion of yoga philosophy and science].

chapter four

Miracles of Healing

Swami Rama spent the last decade of his life building an enormous hospital complex in the Himalayan foothills. It features state-of-the-art medical technology, along with traditional Indian Ayurvedic prescriptions and homeopathy. But much of his life was also devoted to two other important aspects of medical science: preventive medicine and faith healing. The clinics he founded in America helped pioneer the Holistic Health movement in the 1970s and early 1980s, when whole foods and holistic treatment modalities like stress reduction techniques, hatha yoga postures, and meditation were still considered suspicious by many physicians.

Sometimes Swamiji would reminisce about how the yoga masters heal. In the Himalayas these adepts had no access to diagnostic equipment, surgical instruments, or medication. Yet on numerous occasions Swamiji watched these great souls heal desperately ill villagers and mountain people. Through the force of their will, and the faith of the patients who believed in them, these masters routinely performed medical miracles.

In the anecdotes that follow, Swami Rama shares his insights about ancient techniques that really work—and some others that don't—and how faith plays a crucial role in healing.

MY FIRST EXPOSURE TO
THE POWER OF HEALING

*W*hen I was twelve years old, I traveled by foot with my master through the plains of India. We stopped at a railway station in Etah, where my master said to the stationmaster, "My child is with me and he is hungry. Please give us food." The stationmaster went to his home for food, but when he arrived his wife cried, "You know that our only son is suffering from smallpox. How can you be concerned about giving food to these wandering sadhus? My son is dying! Get out of this house! I am in distress."

He returned with a long face and apologized: "What can I do? My wife says, 'If he is a real swami, why doesn't he understand our situation and cure our child? Doesn't he have any sense? Our only child is on his deathbed, and he's worried about a food offering.'"

My master smiled and told me to follow him. We went to the stationmaster's home. It was a challenge, and he always enjoyed being challenged. But I complained, "I am hungry. When are we going to eat?"

He said, "You will have to wait."

This was a frequent complaint of mine. Often I used to cry, "You don't give me food on time." I would run away weeping. But he was teaching me patience.

He said, "You are disturbed now. Wait for five minutes and you won't be disturbed. In this situation it is right to wait." But I continued to complain and the woman wanted to chase me from her house.

It was the first time I had seen someone suffering from smallpox. The boy had big abscesses all over his body, even on his face, with pus draining from them. My master said to the parents, "Don't worry, in two minutes your son will be completely well." He took a glass of water and walked three times around the cot on which the boy was lying. Then he drank the water. He looked at the woman and said, "He's getting well, don't you see?" To our amazement the abscesses began to disappear from the boy, but to my dismay, at the same time they began to appear on my master's face. I was terrified and started to cry.

He said calmly, "Don't worry, nothing will happen to me." Within two minutes the child's face was perfectly clear, and we left the house. I followed him to a banyan tree. He sat under the tree, and soon the abscesses began to disappear from him and to appear on the tree. After ten minutes they also disappeared from the tree. When I saw that my master was all right, I hugged him and wept.

"Don't do that again!" I pleaded. "You didn't look nice, and it frightened me." After that many people started searching for us. I asked, "Have we done anything bad?"

He said, "No, come with me." He held my hand and we started walking again on the bank of the Jamuna River. Finally we stopped at another house and were given food. We then went to an enclosed courtyard where no one could find us, ate our food, and rested.

The sages find pleasure in suffering to help others. This is beyond the conception of the ordinary mind. Human history provides many instances of spiritual leaders who suffered for others. For them it is not suffering, though ordinary people think that they are suffering. When one's consciousness remains limited to the individual boundaries only, then the individual suffers. A great man does not suffer when something happens to his own self but feels more pain in the suffering of others. When individual consciousness expands itself to cosmic consciousness, it becomes easy to feel delight in suffering for the sake of others.

Pain and pleasure are a pair of opposites experienced when the senses contact objects of the world. Those whose consciousness has expanded beyond the sensory level attain freedom from this pair of opposites. There are techniques for voluntarily withdrawing the mind from the senses and focusing inward to reveal the center of consciousness. In such a state of mind one is not affected by sensory pleasure or pain. Such a one-pointed mind also creates a dynamic will, which can be used for healing others. All such healing powers flow through the human being from the one source of consciousness. The moment the healer becomes conscious of his individuality, that spontaneous flow of healing power stops. Healing is a natural power in man. The healing of others is possible through that willpower that is not interrupted by the lower mind.

My Master Sends Me to Heal Someone

*O*ne fine morning my master and I were sitting outside our cave when suddenly he said, "You have to catch a bus. The bus route is seven miles from here, so hurry up." He often told me to get up and go somewhere on the spur of the moment. Sometimes I wouldn't know why, but I would find out when I reached there. I rose and picked up the pot of water I always carried. He said, "Take the bus to the Haridwar railroad station. You'll get a ticket, and from there go to Kanpur. Dr. Mitra is bedridden and is constantly remembering me. He is having a brain hemorrhage and is bleeding out of his right nostril, but his wife will not allow him to go to the hospital. His brother-in-law, Dr. Basu, knows that it is a hemorrhage, but there are no facilities there to perform brain surgery."

I asked, "What shall I do?"

"Just give him a love pat on the cheek. Don't consider yourself a healer. Think that you are an instrument and go there, for I have promised him and his wife that we will always help them. Go as quickly as you can."

I said, "I'm surprised to find that you make promises on my behalf without my knowledge." I was reluctant to go on such a long journey, but I could not disobey. I went to the bus route, which was seven miles away from the cave, and stood by the side of the road until the bus for Rishikesh and Haridwar picked me up. The drivers would always give a swami a ride when they saw one on the roadside. I got off the bus at the railway station at Haridwar with no money, and I had only half an hour until the train was to leave for Kanpur. I looked at my watch and thought I might be able to sell it to buy a ticket.

Approaching a gentleman at the railway station, I asked if I could exchange my watch for the money to buy a ticket. Surprisingly he said, "My son could not come with me, so I have an extra ticket. Please take it. I don't need your watch."

I got on the train and met a lady who was also going to Kanpur and who was a close relative of Dr. Mitra. She had heard about me and my master from Dr. Mitra and his wife, and she gave me food to eat. We traveled all night, and in the morning the train arrived at Kanpur. There was so much rush at the railway station that it took me ten minutes to get through the gate. Outside the station I unexpectedly met a man who knew me well. He had his car parked nearby and had been waiting for someone, but that person had missed his train in Delhi. This man wanted to drive me to his house, but I insisted that we go to Dr. Mitra's instead.

When we reached there I found three doctors examining Dr. Mitra. Mrs. Mitra was delighted to see me and said, "Now that you have come, I hand over my husband to you."

I said, "I am not a healer. I have just come to see him." I went to Dr. Mitra's bed, but he was not allowed to sit up because of the bleeding from his nostril.

When he saw me he asked, "How is my master?" I gave

him the gentle pat on his right cheek. After a few minutes there was no more bleeding. One of the doctors explained that the slap I had given him on the cheek closed the opening in the blood vessel and that it was now sealed.

I did not know what I had done, but I followed my master's instructions. Dr. Mitra's sudden recovery quickly became the talk of the town, and hundreds of patients started searching for me, so I left the city later that day and reached Haridwar the next morning. From there I went to the place where my master was staying. I told my master teasingly, "I know the secret and can stop a hemorrhage in anyone."

He laughed at me and said, "The doctor who gave you that explanation is quite ignorant. There are various modes and levels of suffering, but ignorance is the mother of them all."

A human being is fully equipped with all necessary healing powers, but he doesn't know how to use them. A human being is only an instrument. All the powers belong to God.

UNORTHODOX WAYS OF HEALING

The belief in possession is as old as the oldest cultures. We still hear about possessions by a demon or ghost or spirit. All over the world I have found that not only ignorant people but also educated priests believe in the reality of possession. But this possession is just a mental imbalance. It is possible to treat such cases with religious rituals and ceremonies. In most communities of the world, such rituals are still practiced, though sometimes clandestinely. In most of the cases that I had an opportunity to examine, the problem was hysteria, usually caused by sexual repression. There are other causes, such as pathological fear of losing something or of not being able to obtain something that is desperately desired.

There are certain places in India where patients are brought to be freed from a "possession." The "therapists" use crude methods, including whipping the patient before an idol. During the treatment one of the therapists, called a *vakya,* comes forward as though he were also possessed, but by a deva (good spirit). Sometimes, while in a highly concentrated state of emotion, the vakya jumps into the flames of a fire to prove how mighty his powers are. Then, chanting hymns, he tries to help the patient out of his condition. There are many such practitioners scattered throughout the Himalayan mountains.

Once in 1945 a neurologist from Australia came to see me at my mountain home and stayed with me for ten days. There were few hospitals or dispensaries in the mountains at that time. I had hoped that this man could help the villagers by prescribing a few medicines. His reason for coming to the Himalayas to see me was to find a way to heal his severe chronic headaches, which prevented him from leading a normal life. Although he was a doctor himself and had been examined by many other doctors, he could not find the cause of the headaches, and no one had been able to successfully treat him.

An old woman who used to bring milk to my cabin smiled when she saw him and said, "Is he a doctor?" She laughed and said to me, "If I am permitted, I can remove his headache in two minutes."

I said, "Please try."

She brought one of the herbs that is well known and widely used in the mountains for making fire. A spark made by friction between two rocks ignites the herb. She crushed the herb and put a bit of it on the doctor's right temple and said, "Believe me, you will be free from headaches forever. Lie down." When he did so, she placed an iron hook in the fire and heated the point until it was red. Then she put the red-hot point on the herb, which had been placed on his temple. The doctor screamed and jumped up. I also was shocked. The woman calmly returned to her village, and the doctor's headaches were gone.

Such treatments are often used by the villagers. The doctor said, "Which science is this? I want to learn more about it." I did not encourage him, for although I believe that occasionally such treatments may help, they are not systematic, and it is very difficult to evaluate which ones are truly effective and which are only a matter of super-stition. The doctor persisted, though, and left for the Garhwal mountains, where he studied under a mountain medicine man, Vaidya Bhairavdutt, who knew more than three thousand varieties of herbs. When the doctor met me again six months later he reported, "I know the explanation of that treatment I received from the old lady. It is based on the principles that were used by travelers who went across the Tibetan border to China and that have been systematized as acupuncture. Charaka, the ancient Indian master of medicine, mentions it as *suchi vedha, sui* in modern Hindi, the needle-pricking treatment."

I concluded that he had been relieved of one kind of headache but was now creating a new headache for himself by investigating these cures. There are many things known to the villagers that work, but we would be wise not to adopt them until we understand their underlying principles.

Herbs and medicine prepared from metals are not in common use in the West today. Although we have many modern means to prepare drugs, drugs are not the remedy for all diseases. Ayurveda [the indigenous Indian medical system] uses herbs and many other methods of treatment. Water therapy, clay therapy, steam therapy, color therapy, sun baths, and the use of juices of various fruits, flowers, and vegetables are essential components of Ayurvedic therapy. The Ayurvedic method of treating disease is divided into two sections: *nidana* [recognizing the factors that create ill health] and *pathya* [a regimen prescribed to cure a disease]. Therapists prescribe changes in eating, sleeping, and even climate, instead of putting patients in the terrifying conditions often found in crowded modern hospitals.

I have often wondered how the people of the Himalayas stay so healthy and live so long, though they enjoy few of the benefits of modern medicine. There are many diseases for which modern medical science has not discovered a remedy, but these mountaineers do not suffer from them. Perhaps fresh food, fresh air, and, above all, free thinking with no anxiety is responsible for their health. Millions of patients all over the world who suffer from psychosomatic diseases can be helped through right diet, juices, relaxation, breathing, and meditation. Preventive and alternative medicine should not be ignored.

HEALING IN A HIMALAYAN SHRINE

A party of businessmen and a few doctors decided to visit the shrine of Badrinath in the Himalayas. Mr. Jaipuria, a prominent businessman from Kanpur, organized this pilgrimage, and Dr. Sharma went along to serve as health custodian to the forty people in the party. They insisted that I go with them to teach the group. With the exception of the organizer, who was carried in a palanquin, we went on foot from Karnaprayag, and after several day's journey reached Badrinath. By that time, since they were not used to walking in the mountains, all the members of the party were worn out and tired and suffered from aches and pains. Upon reaching Badrinath everyone rushed for a bath in the hot springs. My room was on the quiet side of a big building that housed travelers. I was in the habit of remaining awake at night and resting from one o'clock to three thirty in the afternoon.

At two thirty in the morning, Mr. Jaipuria knocked at my door and said, "Swamiji, please come out! My brother is suffering a severe heart attack and the doctors cannot handle it. Please help now!"

Mr. Jaipuria loves me very much, but I strictly maintain that early period of the morning for meditation, and this distraction was a disturbance to my willpower. I also knew that there were several doctors there with oxygen and medical kits, so rather than open the door, I said from inside, "We yogis and swamis aspire to die in a place like this, and it never happens. How can it be possible for your brother to have chosen such an auspicious place to die? It is not possible; he is not dying. Go away and don't disturb me." I found Jaipuria's brother quite normal in the morning. This retort of mine became a joke among the businessmen: "If the holy men are not fortunate enough to die in a shrine like Badrinath, how is it possible for businessmen to have such a peaceful death? It's not possible!"

The next morning everyone went to the shrine and met many swamis who lived in nearby caves. At five o'clock in the evening Dr. Sharma, the head physician of the party, told me that Mrs. Jaipuria was suffering from bloody diarrhea. She was a fine little old lady who always looked after my comfort. I called her Mother. I felt sad and rushed to see her. Her face was very pale, and she was so completely exhausted that she could move only her lips. Her two sons sitting next to her did not believe that she would live. The doctor gave her medication to no avail. Her breath was shallow, and the doctors declared her case hopeless. I put my hand over her head in sympathy. I did not know what to do. Suddenly I turned my head and saw a tall young swami calling my name. This swami said, "Where is the doctor?" and the doctor came forward. Then he said, "That's all your medical science can do? You are killing people and drugging them. What poor knowledge!"

The doctor was annoyed and told him, "How is it that you two swamis cannot heal her? I accept that I have failed and that the other doctors have also failed."

Mr. Jaipuria loved his wife immensely and was sobbing in a corner of the room. His sons and in-laws were also crying. I looked at the young swami, and he smiled and asked for a flower. People carry flowers to offer at the shrine, so someone came forward with the red petals of roses. The swami told Mrs. Jaipuria to get up. He roughly pulled her arm, forcibly made her sit, and poured a glass of water containing the petals into her mouth while muttering something that nobody understood. He then laid her on the bed, covered her with the blanket, and told all the people to get out of the room, saying, "She will be going into deep sleep now."

Everyone thought that "deep sleep" meant dying, and they started screaming and crying. We were both smiling at them. This was not at all appreciated, and the old lady's son said, "You irresponsible people have nothing to lose, but I have lost my mother and now you are making fun of me!" The young swami and I stood outside the house and waited for the woman to wake up, while her family members prepared for her cremation. After half an hour the young swami asked Mr. Jaipuria to go inside and be with his wife. He found her sitting up and in perfectly good health.

I am not against medicines and remedies that help in curing diseases, but I love to make others aware of preventive medicine. There is another, higher, way of helping people through the use of willpower. Willpower means that dynamic will that is created by a one-pointed mind, meditation, and spiritual discipline. In today's medicine this cultivation of willpower is totally missing.

The young swami accepted the doctor's challenge and was aware of his potential to heal the suffering old lady. My experience with many medical professionals has convinced me that in treating diseases, the doctor's behavior and willpower is more important than mere medication. The more the medical profession understands this fact, the more they will understand that they can help humanity not only by using medicine but also by teaching methods of prevention. In this way more patients can be aware of their inner capacities to heal themselves.

THE HIMALAYAN HEALERS

I went to Kasardevi in Almora, and there I met a well-known painter from the West and a Buddhist monk. They lived in a small hermitage, enjoying the Himalayan peaks in solitude. They talked to the mountains constantly and held that the Himalayan mountains, unlike the Alps and other mountains, are not only beautiful but alive as well.

They said, "We talk to the mountains and the mountains answer."

I asked, "In what sense? How can mountains talk?"

They replied, "You were born and brought up in these mountains, and, as always, familiarity breeds contempt. Remember that these mountains are holy and create a spiritual atmosphere for the seeker. Their beauty is for all who behold it. You have forgotten how to appreciate these gods." They went on praising the beauty of the snow-blanketed Himalayan peaks.

My stay with them was brief. I soon left for Shyamadevi, thirty miles beyond Kasardevi, where a swami lived all alone in a small shakti temple [a temple to the Divine Mother]. Soon after I arrived, Nantin Baba, a well-known sadhu from that part of the Himalayas, joined us. I had previously lived with him in various caves at Bageswar and Ramgarh. The swami who lived at the shakti temple claimed that he was a direct disciple of Sombari Baba, a well-known sage who lived forty years earlier. During those days Sombari Baba and Hariakhan Baba often were seen together. My master and Hariakhan Baba were disciples of the same guru, who was from India but lived mostly in Tibet. Both Hariakhan Baba and my master were called Babaji. This title of respect simply means "grandfather," and is often used for old sages. Even today, especially in Nepal, Nanital, Kashipur, and Almora, there are many stories about these sages and their amazing spiritual miracles and healing powers. During our stay there our host talked about his *gurudeva* [spiritual mentor] uninterruptedly for hours on end. There is no end to the stories they tell about these sages.

Our host was a *siddha* [yogic adept]. He was widely known for his healing powers. Whenever anyone started traveling to the shakti temple at which he stayed, he knew it. Without being introduced to strangers he would straight away call them by their names. He did not want to be disturbed, and sometimes he would feign anger in order to keep people away, but within he was very soft. Villagers gave him the name Durbasa, which means "foul tongue." He performed a primitive austerity called Panchagni Siddhi, which means having control over five fires. He did both external and internal worship. He said that God is fire, and would expound on this theme given the slightest opportunity.

This accomplished man gave me several lessons on solar science, which I still remember, though I did not practice what he taught me, for it is not possible to practice everything in one short lifetime. This science is helpful in healing the sick. After collecting scattered material on this subject and learning its principles, I wanted to set up a clinic to help the suffering masses, but my master stopped me. He felt this would distract me from an even greater purpose.

When I left Shyamadevi I returned to my mountain abode. The villagers of Budha Kedar built a small stone dwelling for me. It is still there today, at a height of six thousand feet. From that dwelling I had a panoramic view of the Himalayan ranges. Occasionally the silence would be broken by a wandering yogi knocking on my door. Only a few seekers go deep into the Himalayas. Most travelers remain on the roads and trails and visit the well-known shrines, but the more serious seekers avoid these routes and visit the isolated hermitages and caves of sages. The Himalayas stretch for fifteen hundred miles from China to Pakistan. They are the highest mountains in the world. Though there are other beautiful mountain ranges, the Himalayas offer one thing that is unique: a spiritual atmosphere and the opportunity to meet and learn from the highly evolved sages who make the Himalayas their home.

chapter five

Trusting the Extraordinary

India is famous for its mysterious yogic sciences. To offer just one of many examples, yogis use mantras (empowered words, sounds, and affirmations) to alter their consciousness, and sometimes to alter reality itself. Usually these sciences are carefully guarded secrets, as their misuse can lead to serious problems.

During his years in the mountains, Swami Rama mastered numbers of these hidden sciences, which he would occasionally demonstrate for us to prove their authenticity. The demonstrations he performed at the Menninger Foundation in the early 1970s turned Western science on its head. Though the results were published in scientific journals as well as the press, it took decades for the full implications of these findings to seep into Western scientific culture. Yet Swamiji often expressed disappointment that the researchers at Menninger had asked him to show them only the most basic of yogic skills. Abilities of far more value, such as the ability to enter very high states of consciousness at will or to transmute matter or read minds—much less to remain permanently in a state of enlightenment beyond pain and fear—were still so far beyond Western science that researchers refused to even design experiments to test for them. Why test for yogic skills the scientists believed couldn't possibly exist?

We in the West have shortchanged ourselves by refusing to explore the inner worlds. We've drawn an artificial line segregating physics from metaphysics—a false distinction Eastern cultures refused to make. As a consequence our science is soulless, and our understanding of how the living universe operates is woefully stunted.

In this chapter Swami Rama will introduce you to some of the vidyas or yogic sciences. This brief glimpse is in fact a glimmering of the higher truths of our own inner nature.

When we gain faith that this inner world exists, and that through disciplined effort we can enter this world just as Swami Rama did, then an entire, previously unsuspected, universe of spirit opens up before us.

A Mantra for Happiness

A mantra is a syllable, a sound, a word, or set of words revealed to the great sages in a deep state of meditation. It is not the language in which human beings speak. Those sounds that are received from the superconscious state lead the seeker higher and higher until he reaches perfect silence. The more awareness increases, the more the mantra reveals new meaning. It makes one aware of a higher dimension of consciousness.

A mantra is exactly like a human being. It has many sheaths—gross, subtle, more subtle, and subtlest. For example, take *Aum*. These three letters represent the three states (waking, dreaming, and sleeping) or the three bodies (gross, subtle, and more subtle). But the fourth state or the finest body of the mantra is formless, soundless, and indefinable. A student, if he understands the process of Laya Yoga [a form of spiritual practice in which a yogi progressively dissolves the grosser constituents of his nature into the more subtle ones] can know the formless body and superconsciousness of mantra. Mantra is very powerful and essential, a compact form of prayer. If remembered constantly, it becomes a guide.

I used to collect mantras like people collect material objects, hoping that some new mantra I was about to receive would be better than what I already had. Sometimes I would compare myself to other students and think, "My mantra is better than his mantra." I was very immature.

There was a swami who lived quietly deep in the Himalayas between Uttarkashi and Harsil. I went to see him. When I arrived he asked, "What is the purpose of your coming?" I told him, "I want to receive a mantra."

"You will have to wait," he replied.

When Westerners go to someone for a mantra, they are prepared to spend a lot of money, but they don't want to wait. I tried the same thing. I said, "Swamiji, I am in a hurry."

"Then come next year," he said.

"If I stay now, how many days will I have to wait?" I asked.

"You will have to wait as long as I want you to wait," he replied.

So I waited patiently, one day, two days, three days. Still the swami wouldn't give me a mantra. On the fourth day he said, "I want to give you a mantra, but promise that you will remember it all the time." I promised.

He said, "Let us go to the Ganga." Countless sages have done spiritual practices on the banks of the sacred Ganga and have been initiated there. I stood by the river and said, "I promise I will not forget this mantra." I repeated this promise several times, but he still delayed.

At last he said, "No matter where you live, live cheerfully. This is the mantra. Be cheerful at all times, even if you are behind bars. Anywhere you live, even if you have to go to a hellish place, create heaven there. Remember, my boy, cheerfulness is of your own making. It only requires human effort. You have to create cheerfulness for yourself. Remember this mantra of mine."

I was both very happy and very sad, because I had expected him to give me some unusual sound to repeat. But he was more practical. I apply this "mantra" in my life and find it successful everywhere. His spiritual prescription is the real key for healing oneself.

A Mantra for Bees

An *apta* mantra is a type of mantra that belongs to the particular sage who imparts it. I want to tell you about an experience I had with such a mantra.

There once was a swami who lived in a small hut across the river from Rishikesh. In order to get there, you had to cross the Ganga on a swinging rope bridge. At that time Rishikesh was not overly populated. Wild elephants sometimes came at night and ate the straw from the walls and roof of our huts. While we were sitting inside they would come in big herds of thirty or forty and would sometimes eat half of a hut. Tigers also roamed about. It was still quite wild.

Following my master's directions, I went to stay with that swami across the river. Early in the morning Swamiji would go for a dip in the Ganga, and I would go with him, for I was expected to follow the customs wherever I stayed. After our baths we would take the twig of a tree, crush its end, and make it into a brush to clean our teeth. We would do this every day. Swamiji's disciple would climb up a tall tree and pull off a branch to make the toothbrushes.

One day Swamiji climbed the tree himself. He didn't usually do that, but this time he wanted to show me something. He was over seventy years old, but he climbed the tree easily. There was a hive of wild bees in that tree, but he made no effort to avoid it. On the contrary, he climbed up to that very branch and started talking to the bees. From down below I shouted, "Swamiji, please don't disturb the bees!" I covered my head because I thought, "If they are disturbed, they will also sting me." They were large and dangerous bees, so dangerous, in fact, that if ten or twenty were to sting you, you might not survive.

The swami pulled off a branch right by the hive, but the bees were not aroused. He came down safely and said, "Now you go up and pluck a branch for yourself."

I replied, "I don't need one. I can live without it." Then I added, "If you want me to climb the tree, first tell me the mantra that protected you." During that time I was fascinated with mantras, and I wanted to know his mantra because I wanted to show people what I could do. That was my purpose.

The swami said that if I climbed the tree he would tell me the mantra, so I climbed up to the hive. He said, "Go nearer and talk to them face to face. Say, 'I live here alongside you and I don't harm you. Don't harm me!'"

I said to Swamiji, "That is not a mantra."

He replied, "Do as I say. Talk to the bees. Your lips should be so close you can whisper to them."

I asked, "How do they know Hindi?"

He answered, "They know the language of the heart, so they know all the languages—just talk to them."

I was skeptical, but I did exactly as he instructed, and I was surprised that the bees did not attack me. I said, "Swamiji, are they tame?"

He laughed and said, "Don't impart this mantra to anyone, for it will work only for you. Don't forget what I am telling you."

Later when I traveled to more populated areas I would usually stay outside the city in a garden, and people would come to see me there. I was young and immature and wanted to boast. I would climb a tree and casually take some honey from a hive without incurring a single sting. It was always a surprising feat.

When I was in Bhiwani, Punjab, a goldsmith whom I knew well requested, "Please give me the mantra." I agreed, forgetting that the swami told me it would not work for anyone else. I told him how to talk to the bees. He climbed up to a hive and repeated the mantra, but it didn't work. The bees attacked him—hundreds of bees at once. He fell from the tree and we rushed him to the hospital, where he remained in a coma for three days. I was worried, thinking, "Suppose I have killed this poor man." I prayed continuously that he would be spared.

On the third day I was astonished to see the swami who had given me the mantra appear at the hospital. He said, "What have you done? By showing off you have nearly killed someone. Let this be a final lesson to you. The man will recover in the morning, but I am withdrawing the power of this mantra from you. You can never use it again." Since that time I have been more cautious. Sometimes the words of a great man can have the effect of a mantra. Whenever a truly great man speaks to you, you should accept his words as mantras and practice them.

MISUSE OF MANTRA

There are some manuscripts in the monastery to which access is strictly prohibited. No one is allowed to read them except the head of the monastery. They are called Prayoga Shastras, and they describe advanced practices.

My master told me, "You are not to experiment with those manuscripts." But I was obstinate and eager to know what was written in them. I was eighteen years old, fearless but somewhat irresponsible. I thought, "I am quite advanced. Why did they write these manuscripts if they are to be left unused? I should do experiments with the practices in these manuscripts. My master is powerful; he will protect me if anything goes wrong."

My master gave me one of these manuscripts to carry for him on a journey. He said, "Do not open it."

I was very curious and resolved, "If he leaves this manuscript with me and I find myself alone, I am going to read it."

One evening we came upon a small dwelling on a bank of the Ganga. My master went inside the hut to rest. I thought, "Here is my chance to study the manuscript." There were no windows and only one door in the little dwelling. I locked the door from the outside. I thought that I would spend the whole night reading the manuscript. It was a moonlit night and I could see clearly. The manuscript was wrapped and tied with a string. I took my time unwrapping it and then started reading. It described a certain practice and the effects it would produce.

After reading for an hour I thought, "Why not try it?" The manuscript said that only advanced yogis should do this practice, and that if it were not done properly it was dangerous. But I thought I was very advanced, so I put the manuscript aside and started doing the practice. It involved repeating a special mantra in a particular style with certain rituals. That mantra awakens a power outside of a person as well as inside.

The manuscript said that the mantra had to be repeated 1,001 times. I repeated it 900 times and nothing seemed to be happening. I concluded there would be no effect. But when I came to 940, I saw a huge woman nearby. She was gathering wood and started making a fire. Then she put water in a big vessel and put it on the fire to boil. By then I had counted to 963. The last I counted was 970, and after that I lost track because I saw a huge man coming from the same direction. At first I thought, "This must be the effect of the mantra. I won't look at him, and complete the 1,001 repetitions." But he started coming toward me. I had never before seen or even imagined such a gigantic man, and he was completely nude.

He asked the woman, "What have you cooked for me?"

She said, "I have nothing. If you give me something, I'll cook it."

He pointed at me and said, "Look at him sitting over there. Why don't you cut him into pieces and cook him?"

When I heard that, my teeth clenched and the mala I was counting with fell from my hand. I fainted. I don't know how long I remained unconscious. When I regained consciousness my master was standing in front of me. He slapped me on the cheek and said, "Hey, wake up." I would become conscious momentarily and exclaim, "Oh, that giant is going to carve me up!" and then lapse into a faint again.

This happened three or four times, until finally my master kicked me, became more insistent, and said, "Get up! Why have you done this? I told you not to practice these mantras. And you locked me in, you foolish boy."

From this experience I realized the power of mantra. I started practicing the mantra my master had given me and I began to count on it even for little things. I did many foolish and silly things when I was young, but my mantra, which created awareness for me, always helped me to come out of those situations.

If mantra is not properly used with spiritual discipline, it can lead to hallucinations, as it did for me. Hallucinations are the products of an impure and

untrained mind. Mantra becomes helpful when the mind
is purified and directed inward.

BLACK MAGIC

My brother disciple, whose father was a learned
Sanskrit pandit, was from Medanipur, Bengal. When he
was eighteen years old, before I had met him, his family
forced him to get married. The marriage ceremony was
being performed in the evening, and this suited his plans
well. During a Hindu wedding the bride and groom par-
ticipate in a fire ceremony and take seven steps around
the fire. On the fourth step he jumped out of the ritual and
ran into the fields. The people in the wedding party did
not understand his behavior. They began to chase him but
could not catch him. He walked for several days until he
reached the banks of the Ganga and started following the
river in search of a spiritual teacher. For six years he went
through many experiences but did not find a teacher.
Then he met my master at Shrinagar, in the Himalayas.
When they met, my master embraced him and knew that
they had known each other in the past. My brother disciple lived with my master for three months and then was
sent to Gangotri, where we stayed in a cave together.

One day he began talking about his hometown,
Medanipur, and told me that if ever I visited there I should
tell his family that he had become a renunciate and lives in
the Himalayas. Soon after that I visited his home and met

the woman to whom he was to have been married. She was waiting for him to come home. I suggested to her that she marry someone else because the marriage ceremony had not been completed. On hearing this advice from me, she said, "You and your brother disciple are the worshippers of the devil and not of God." She was in a fit of anger.

I went back to my hut, which was situated outside the village. In that area tantra was practiced. I had heard much about tantra and had read a few scriptures. I wanted to meet someone who could really demonstrate the practices so that I would have no doubts of their validity. One of my brother disciple's cousins in that village introduced me to a ninety-two-year-old Mohammedan tantric. I went to see him and we talked for three hours. He was famous as a *maulavi,* a priest who leads the prayers in the mosques and knows the Koran, the sacred bible of Islam.

The next morning the maulavi took me to a pond outside the village. He also brought a chicken. First he tied this chicken with a string and then he tied the other end of the string to a banana plant. He told me to sit down and watch attentively. He was muttering something and throwing black-eyed peas on the string. The chicken fluttered and became lifeless. He said, "The chicken is dead."

I thought, "This is not being creative. It is a very bad power. It's black magic." He asked me to make sure that the chicken was dead. I said, "Can I put the chicken underwater for some time?"

He said, "Go ahead."

I kept the chicken underwater for more than five minutes and then took it out. To my knowledge the chicken was dead. Then he brought the chicken back to life by performing that same ritual of throwing black-eyed peas and muttering something. This really shook me up. He said, "Now tie one end of the string on the banana plant and tie the other end to your waist. I'll show you something different."

Instead of doing what he said, I ran as fast as I could toward the village, leaving the old maulavi and his chicken far behind. When I arrived I was breathless, and the villagers did not know why I was running so fast. I told them that the old maulavi wanted to kill me, but no one believed me, for in that area he was considered to be a holy man. I thought, "I'd better leave this place and tread my path instead of seeking miracles."

From there I went to Calcutta to stay a few days with the chief justice, R. P. Mukharji. When I told him of my experience and asked if I had imagined it or hallucinated, he said, "No, such things happen." Later I asked some sages how such a miracle was accomplished. They could not explain it but acknowledged that Bengal was famous for such practices. When I related this story to my master, he laughed at me and said, "You need exposure to all sorts of things, although you should not attempt to practice them yourself. You should follow only that discipline that has been given to you."

This sort of tantra is an offshoot, not the real science of

tantra. The power of the mind can be used in many ways. Without knowledge of the goal of life, mental faculties can be directed negatively for harming others. But ultimately this misuse of mental powers destroys the person who practices it. There still exist a few people with such tantric powers. But out of a hundred, one is genuine and the other ninety-nine are magicians.

THE THIEF

In my youth I searched for miracles. Once when I saw a person lying on a bed of nails, I said to him, "I wish I could do that. Can you teach me?"

He said, "Of course. But first you will have to beg alms for me and bring money to me. If you promise that you will give me whatever money you have, I will teach you!"

One after another I met many such people and they despised each other, saying, "He is nothing. I will teach you something better." One of them had a big steel needle, and he pushed it through his arm. He said, "See, there is no bleeding. I will teach you this, and you'll be able to make money by demonstrating it to others. But you will have to become my disciple and give me a part of what you earn."

I left him and went to another person. Many people respected this man. I wanted to know why so many people followed him. I wondered, "What exclusive knowledge does he have? Is he wise? Is he a great yogi?"

I stayed with him until everyone went away. When I

was all alone with him, he asked, "Which is the most luxurious hotel that you know of?"

I said, "The Savoy Hotel in London."

He said, "You pay me one hundred rupees and I will get you some delicious food from the restaurant of that hotel." I gave him a hundred rupees and suddenly some food appeared before me, exactly as it was prepared at that hotel. Next I asked for some food from Hamburg, Germany. Again I paid him seventy rupees and he got the dish I requested. It appeared along with the bill.

I thought, "Why should I go back to my master? I'll stay with this man and all my needs will be taken care of. Then without any bother, I can quietly meditate and study."

He asked, "What type of watch do you want?"

I replied, "I already have a good watch." But he said, "I will give you a better watch," and he did it.

When I looked at the watch I thought, "This watch is manufactured in Switzerland. He is not creating these things; he is only doing a trick, transporting them from one place to another."

Two weeks later I went to him again and bowed before him. I gave him an oil massage and helped him cook food. He was pleased with this and he instructed me, so I could do things similar to those he had done. I practiced until one of the swamis from our monastery came and slapped me, saying, "What are you doing?" He took me to my master, who said, "You have committed many thefts."

I asked, "What thefts?"

He answered, "You ask for sweets and they come to you from someone's shop. They disappear from the shop and the owner does not know what has happened to them." I promised my master that I would never do this again.

Later I met a man who worked as a salesman in a store that sold sewing machines in Delhi. I told him about the *haji* [wonder worker] and his powers. The salesman said, "If he can get a Singer sewing machine from my store in Delhi, I will consider him to be the greatest man alive and follow him for the rest of my life."

So we both went to him and requested him to perform the miracle. He said, "I will get it immediately," and it appeared! Then the salesman became concerned that it would be missing from the store and he might be accused of stealing it. The haji tried to send it back, but he could not do so. He started weeping and crying, "I've lost my powers!"

When the salesman returned to Delhi, he took the machine with him. In the meantime at the store, they had discovered the machine was missing, and they reported the matter to the police. The police found it in the salesman's possession and he was taken to the court. No one believed his story and the salesman was punished.

I had many such experiences and I insulted my master many times by saying, "There are people who have powers greater than yours, so I want to follow them." He said, "Go ahead! I want you to grow and be great. You don't have to follow me!"

Later I realized that most such phenomena are tricks.

Wherever they are found to be genuine, they are black magic. Spirituality has nothing to do with these miracles. The third chapter of the *Yoga Sutra* explains many methods of attaining siddhis, but these siddhis create stumbling blocks in the path of enlightenment. One person in millions does indeed have siddhis, but I have found that such people are often greedy, egotistical, and ignorant. The path of enlightenment is different from the intentional cultivation of powers. The miracles performed by Buddha, Christ, and other great sages were spontaneous and for a purpose. They were not performed with selfish motives or to create a sensation.

On the path of yoga one may come across the potential of acquiring siddhis. A yogi without having any desire for a siddhi might get one, but one who is aware of the purpose of his life never misuses them. Misuse of siddhis is the downfall of a yogi.

A FIRE-THROWER SWAMI

I once met a swami who could produce fire from his mouth. The flame would shoot out several feet. I tested him to see if the phenomenon was authentic. I asked him to wash out his mouth, to be sure he was not hiding something like phosphorus in it. I also had my friends examine him. He seemed genuine, so I concluded, "This man must definitely be more advanced than my master."

That swami said to me, "You are wasting your time

and energy staying with your master. Follow me and I will give you some real wisdom. I will show you how to produce fire."

I was so swayed by him that I decided to leave my master. I went to my master and said, "I have found someone more advanced than you, and I have decided to become his disciple."

He said, "I am delighted. Go ahead, I want you to be happy. What does he do?"

I replied, "He produces fire from his mouth. He is a very powerful swami."

My master requested, "Please take me to him."

The next morning we went. The swami was staying twenty-three miles away in the mountains and it took us two days to get there. When we arrived, the swami bowed before my master! I was surprised and asked my master, "Do you know him?"

He replied, "Of course. He left our monastery some time ago. Now I know where he has been hiding." My master asked him, "What have you been doing here?"

He said, "Sir, I have learned to produce fire from my mouth."

When my master saw the flame come from his mouth, he laughed gently. He instructed me, "Ask him how many years it has taken to learn this." That swami was proud of his accomplishment.

He bragged, "I have practiced twenty years to master this."

Then my master said to me, "A match will produce fire

in a second; if you wish to spend twenty years to produce fire from your mouth, you are a fool. My child, that is not wisdom. If you really want to meet masters, I'll give you directions to where they are staying. Go and have the experiences."

Later I realized that all such siddhis are but mere signs on the path. These psychic powers have nothing to do with spirituality and have little value. On the contrary, they can create serious obstacles on the path. Sometimes psychic powers develop—you start telling the fortunes of others, you start knowing things. These are all distractions. Do not allow them to obstruct your path. Too many people, including swamis, have wasted time and energy on such distractions. Anyone who wants to develop siddhis can do so, and can demonstrate certain supernatural feats; but enlightenment is an entirely different matter.

THE WAVE OF BLISS

I once met a handsome swami who was highly educated in the Vedantic and yoga tradition. He knew the scriptures and was a brilliant *sadhaka* [spiritual practitioner]. He was later nominated as Shankaracharya of Jyotirmayapitham, which is in the Himalayas on the way to Badrinath. His name was Brahmananda Sarasvati.

He lived on a hillock in a small natural cave near a mountain pool and ate only germinated gram seeds mixed with a little salt. I was led by the villagers to that place, but I was disappointed not to find him there. The next day I went again, and found a few footprints made by his wooden sandals on the edge of the pool. I tried, but I could not track the footprints. Finally on the fifth day, early in the morning before sunrise, I went back to the pool and found him taking a bath. I greeted him saying, "Namo Narayan," which is a commonly used salutation among swamis, meaning "I bow to the divinity in you." He was observing silence, so he motioned for me to follow him to his small cave. This was the eighth day of his silence, and after staying the night with him, he broke his silence and I gently spoke to him about the purpose of my visit. I wanted to know how he was living and the methods of his spiritual practices.

He talked to me about Sri Vidya, the highest of paths, followed only by accomplished Sanskrit scholars of India. It is a path that joins Raja Yoga [the "royal path" of yoga taught by Patanjali in the *Yoga Sutra*], Kundalini Yoga [spiritual practice that involves controlling the energies of the subtle body], Bhakti Yoga [love for God], and Advaita Vedanta [intellectual inquiry leading to intuitive realization]. There are two books recommended by the teachers of this path: *The Wave of Bliss* and *The Wave of Beauty*. In Sanskrit the compilation of these two books is called *Saundaryalahari*. Another part of this literature, the *Prayoga Shastra,* is in manuscript form and found only in the Mysore and Baroda libraries. No scholar can understand these spiritual yoga poems without the help of a competent teacher who himself practices these teachings.

Later on I found that Sri Vidya and Madhu Vidya are spiritual practices known to a very few—only ten to twelve people in all of India. I became interested in knowing this science, and whatever little I have today is because of it. In this science the body is seen as a temple and the indweller, Atman, as God. A human being is like a miniature universe, and by understanding this, one can understand the whole of the universe and ultimately realize the absolute One.

In this path the kundalini fire is seen as the Mother Divine, and through yoga practices it is awakened from its primal state and raised to the highest of the chakras. The chakras are wheels of life that form our spiritual body and connect the entire flow of consciousness. The science of chakra is very terse, but if one knows this science well it serves him on all levels. The chakras operate on the physical, physiological, energetic, mental, and spiritual levels. These energy centers correspond in the physical body to points along the spinal cord. The lowest is located at the coccyx, the second in the sacral area, the third at the navel, the fourth at the heart, the fifth at the base of the throat, the sixth at the point between the eyebrows, and the seventh at the crown of the head. The lowest chakras are the grooves toward which the lower mind rushes.

The heart *(anahata)* chakra separates the upper hemisphere from the lower hemisphere and is accepted as the center of divine tranquility. Buddhism, Hinduism,

Christianity, and Judaism also recognize this center. The anahata chakra in Hinduism is the Star of David in Judaism and the Sacred Heart in Christianity. The higher chakras are the centers of upward-traveling energy. There are many levels of consciousness from the heart chakra to the thousand-petalled lotus inside the crown of the head. When one sits erect for meditation these centers are aligned. Energy can be focused on one chakra or another. Developing the capacity to direct the flow of energy to the higher chakras is one aspect of spiritual development. Knowledge of pranic vehicles [subtle bodies composed of vital force] is important if one wants to experience all the chakras systematically.

Swami Brahmananda was one of the rare siddhas [accomplished ones] who had knowledge of Sri Vidya. It is interesting to note how the great sages direct all their spiritual, mental, and physical resources toward their ultimate goal. Among all the swamis of India, I met only a few who radiated such brilliance and yet lived in the public, remaining unaffected by worldly temptations and distractions. I stayed with him for only a week and then left for Uttarkashi.

chapter six

Encounters with the Divine

So many of us are afraid to be alone. We exorcise the eerie sense of stillness by turning on the radio, the television, the CD player. The computer keeps us company if no one else will. When we turn off all the lights at night, it's comforting to see the streetlights filtering in through the window shades, keeping ghosts and thieves at bay.

But are we really ever completely alone? Are there protective forces that surround us at every moment, if we could only see with the eyes of faith?

As a young man, Swami Rama would wander the mountains and forests of northern India with nothing more than the clothes on his back and a pot for carrying water. He had to contend with wild animals, dangerous terrain, freezing temperatures, avalanches—all the difficulties nature could place in his way. Yet he continually surrendered himself to the power that guided him on his spiritual quest. His faith was not unrewarded. Again and again nature reached out to protect her son.

"Self-surrender is the highest and easiest method for

enlightenment. One who has surrendered himself is always protected by the divine power," Swamiji said. And then he told us these stories to prove his words were true.

PROTECTING ARMS

I know many calm and quiet places in the lap of the Himalayas where one can live and meditate without being disturbed. Whenever I get tired, I think of recharging myself by going to the Himalayas for a short period. One of my favorite places for such a retreat is in the district of Garhwal, twelve miles north of Landsdowne, where at the height of sixty-five hundred feet there is a small Shiva temple surrounded by thick fir trees.

In that region nobody eats corn without offering it to the deity of that temple. According to the local folklore, if people forget to make this offering, their house starts shaking and they behave strangely. When I first heard this story at the age of fourteen, I had a desire to visit that temple. I thought that people create such myths out of their imagination and spread stories that are believed by everyone, though they have no basis in reality. I decided to visit that place to see for myself.

It was seven o'clock in the evening as I approached the temple, and it was already dark. I was traveling along the edge of a cliff. I did not have a light with me, and in those days I wore wooden sandals, which were very unstable. I slipped and was at the verge of falling off a steep cliff when suddenly a tall old man dressed in white caught me in his arms and brought me back to the footpath. He said, "This is a holy place and you are fully protected. I will take you to your destination."

He led me along the path for about ten minutes, until we neared a thatched cottage with a torch burning outside. When we came to the stone wall surrounding the cottage, I thought he was walking just behind me, but when I turned to thank him, I could not find him anywhere. I shouted after him, and the sadhu who lived in the cottage heard me and came out. He was pleased to have a guest and told me to follow him to his small room, where a fire was burning. I told the sadhu about the old man who had shown me the path in the dark. I described his appearance and explained how he had saved me from falling off the cliff.

The sadhu started weeping and said, "You were fortunate to encounter that great man. Do you know why I am here? Seven years ago I also lost my way at exactly the same place. It was eleven o'clock at night. The same old man took hold of my arm and brought me to this thatched hut where I now live. I have never seen him again. I call him Siddha Baba. His loving arms also saved me."

The next morning I searched the whole area but did not find any such man. I went to the cliff and saw the marks where I had slipped. It was a dangerous place, and had I fallen, there would have been no chance of survival. Later I talked to the villagers about my experience and they all knew about this siddha. They believe that he protects their women and children in the forest, but none of the villagers have seen him. During that time I was strictly following the austerities and instructions of my master, and I did not possess or carry anything with me. My experience has often confirmed the belief that those who have nothing are cared for by the Divine. I often remember those loving arms that protected me.

The thatched cottage in which the sadhu lived was just a hundred yards from the small Shiva temple. The temple was in a small clearing in the woods surrounded by tall fir trees. That place was highly charged with spiritual vibrations. I learned that a great siddha had lived there six hundred years ago. He instructed and guided those who lived in the area, although he remained in silence. After his death a six-foot-square temple was built where he lived. Inside is a Shiva lingam (an oval-shaped stone, which is a symbol of Shiva). Even today the villagers visit the temple every three months before each new season begins to keep their memories of that great man alive. I stayed in a small room near the temple for several months, remaining alone and practicing silence and austerities.

A few years after my first visit to that temple, some brahmins decided to build a larger, more solid, and more majestic temple in place of the small old temple, which was no longer in good repair. When the laborers began digging around the foundation to remove the old temple, they found that the earth was full of small snakes of various colors. So they started picking up the snakes along with the dirt, and throwing both aside. But the deeper they dug, the more the snakes appeared. An old woman from a nearby village came to the temple each morning and evening. In the evening she walked three miles to the temple to light the lamp inside, and in the morning she came and extinguished it. She had done this regularly for several years. She didn't want the temple to be modified and warned the builders not to disturb it, but the engineer who was in charge of the project didn't pay her any heed. After digging for six days, they found there was no end to the snakes. The more they removed, the more they found. They dug around the Shiva lingam in order to move it but found that it was buried deep in the ground. They dug down eight feet but could not remove it. On the eighth night the engineer had a dream in which the old yogi who had rescued me appeared with his white beard and long gown. He told the engineer that the Shiva lingam was sacred and should not be moved and that the temple should not be enlarged. So the old temple was rebuilt exactly as it had stood for six centuries.

I visited this place again in the spring of 1973 with Swami Ajaya and a small group of students. We stayed there for six days in a small two-story earthen-and-stone house that had been built a few hundred feet from the temple. Another old sadhu lives there now and serves anyone who comes to visit the temple. The place is serene and beautiful. At the top of the tall hills that surround the valley, you can see the long ranges of the Himalayas as though all the snowy peaks are tightly clinging to one another, determined to stand firmly from eternity to eternity.

THE LAND OF *HAMSAS*

*O*f all the places I have visited in my life, I have found none more fascinating than Gangotri. It is a land of the *hamsas* [enlightened men and women], where the mountain peaks are perennially blanketed with snow. When I was young, between thirty and fifty yogis lived there in small caves along both sides of the Ganga. Most of them did not wear any clothes, and some did not even use fire. For three full winters I lived there by myself in a small cave some five hundred yards away from the cave where my brother disciple was staying. I rarely communicated with anyone. Those of us who lived there would see one another from a distance, but no one disturbed anyone else; no one was interested in socializing. That was one of the most fulfilling periods of my life. I spent most of my time doing yoga practices and living on a mixture of wheat and gram. I would soak the wheat and gram, and when it germinated after two days, add a little salt. This was the only food I took.

A sage who was widely respected throughout India lived in a nearby cave. His name was Krishnashram. One night at about twelve o'clock, I was overwhelmed by a deafening sound as if many bombs were exploding. It was an avalanche, very close by. I emerged from my cave to see what had happened. It was a moonlit night and I could see the other bank of the frozen Ganga, where Krishnashram lived. When I saw the path of the avalanche, I concluded that Sri Krishnashram had been buried beneath it. I quickly put on my long Tibetan coat, took a torch, and rushed to his cave. The Ganga there is just a narrow stream, so I crossed it easily. I found his small cave was quite safe and untouched. He was sitting there smiling.

He was not speaking at that time, so he pointed upward and said, "Hm, hm, hm, hm." Then he wrote on a slate: "Nothing can harm me. I have to live for a long time. These noises and avalanches do not frighten me. My cave is protected." Seeing that he was unharmed and in good spirits, I returned to my cave. In the morning when I could see more clearly, I saw that the avalanche had come down on both sides of his cave. The tall fir trees were completely buried. Only his cave remained undamaged.

I often visited Krishnashram from two to five in the afternoon. I would ask him questions, and he would answer on the slate. His eyes glowed like two bowls of fire, and his skin was as thick as an elephant's. He was almost eighty years of age but very healthy. I wondered how he was able to live without any woolens, fire, or protection from the cold.

He had no possessions at all. A swami who lived half a mile up toward Gomukh regularly brought him food. Once a day he ate roasted potatoes and a piece of whole-wheat bread.

Everyone there in Gangotri drank green tea mixed with an herb called ganga tulsi *(Artemisia cina)*. The yogis and swamis whom I met there taught me many things about herbs and their uses, and also discussed the scriptures with me. Those yogis did not like to come down to the plains of India. Every summer a few hundred pilgrims would visit this shrine, which is one of the highest in the Himalayas. In those days they had to walk ninety-six miles in the mountains to reach it. If anyone wants to see first-hand the power of spirit over mind and body, he can find a few rare yogis there even today.

An Atheistic Swami

I once knew a swami who was learned and highly intellectual. He did not believe in the existence of God. He would try to undermine whatever someone else believed with cleverly formulated arguments. Many scholars avoided him, but he and I were good friends. I was attracted to him for his learning and logic. His entire mind and energy were focused on only one thing—how to argue. He was learned and obstinate.

He would say, "I don't know why people don't come to learn from me."

And I would tell him, "You destroy their beliefs and their faith, so why should they come? They are afraid of you."

He was a well-known man. He had written a book in which he attempted to refute all the classical philosophies. It's a good book, a wonderful book for mental gymnastics. It is called *Shat-Dharshana* or *Six Systems of Indian Philosophy*. The Tibetan and Chinese scholars admired him as a logician and invited him to China. They apparently decided that if there was any learned man anywhere in India, it must be this man.

He did not believe in God, yet he was a monk. He used to say that he became a monk to refute and eliminate the order of monks. "They are all fake," he would say. "They are a burden on society. I have found that there is nothing genuine in monasticism, and I am going to tell the world." He vowed that if anyone could convince him that there was a God, he would become that person's disciple.

Once he asked me, "Do you know my vow?"

I replied, "He would be the greatest fool who would take you as a disciple."

He asked, "What do you mean?"

I said, "What can anyone do with your silly mind? You have sharpened your mind in one way, but you have not known any other dimension."

He retorted, "You are the silly one. You also talk of unknown dimensions. This is all rubbish, fantasy."

I prayed to God and said, "No matter what happens, if

I have to lay down my life, I will make this man aware of some deeper truths."

One day I asked, "Have you seen the Himalayas?"

He replied, "No, I never have."

I told him, "In the summer it is pleasant to travel in the mountains. They are beautiful." I was hoping that if he came with me, I would find an opportunity to set him right.

He said, "That's one thing I would love. With such beautiful mountains, why do we need God?"

I thought, "I will force him into a situation where he has to believe." I planned to take him to one of the high mountains. With a small tent and some biscuits and dried fruits we left for Kailas. It was in the month of September, when the snow starts. I firmly believed in God, and I prayed to the Lord to create a situation in which this swami would be helpless and then cry for God's help. I was young and reckless, so I took him on an arduous path. I myself did not know where we were going, so soon we were lost.

I was born in the Himalayas, so I have developed a resistance to cold. A special posture and a breathing technique helped protect me from the cold. But the poor swami shivered painfully because he was unaccustomed to the mountain cold. Out of compassion and to show that I loved him, I gave him my blanket.

I took him up to a height of fourteen thousand feet where he complained, "I can't breathe properly."

I told him, "I don't have any difficulty."

He said, "You are a young man, so it doesn't affect you."

I said, "Don't accept defeat."

Every day he would teach me philosophy and I would charm him by talking about the mountains. I would say, "What a beautiful thing, to be so close to nature."

After we had been walking in the mountains four days, it started snowing. We camped at a height of fifteen thousand feet. We had only a small tent—four feet by five. When it had snowed up to two feet, I said, "Do you know that it will snow seven to eight feet and our tent will be buried, and we will be buried inside the tent?"

"Don't say that!" he exclaimed.

I said, "It is true."

"Can we go back?"

"There is no way, Swamiji."

"What shall we do?"

I replied, "I will pray to God."

He said, "I believe in facts; I do not believe in the silly things you are speaking of."

I said, "By the grace of my God, the snow will stop. If you want to use your philosophy and intelligence to stop it, you are welcome. Just try."

He said, "How will I know if your prayers work? Suppose you pray and the snow stops. Even then I won't believe in God, because the snow might have stopped anyway."

The snow was soon four feet deep on all sides of the small tent, and he started to feel suffocated. I would make a hole in the snow so we could breathe, but it would soon close again. I knew that something was sure to happen. Either we would die, or he would believe in God.

Finally it happened. He said, "Do something! Your master is a great man, and I have insulted him many times. Perhaps that is why I am now being put through this torture and danger." He started to become frightened.

I said, "If you pray to God, in five minutes the snow will stop and there will be sunshine. If you don't, you will die and you will kill me too. God has whispered this to me."

He asked, "Really? How are you hearing this?"

I said, "He is speaking to me."

He began to believe me. He said, "If there is no sunshine, I am going to kill you, because I am breaking my vow. I have only one basic unconditional vow, and that is not to believe in God."

Under pressure of the fear of death, such a man reverses himself and quickly acquires great devotion. He started praying with tears in his eyes. And I thought, "If the snow doesn't stop in five minutes, then he will harden his heart even more." So I also prayed.

By the grace of God, in exactly five minutes the snow stopped and the sun started to shine. He was surprised— and so was I!

He asked, "Will we live?"

I said, "Yes, God wants us to live."

He said, "Now I realize that there really must be something that I did not understand."

After that, he vowed to live in silence for the rest of his life. He lived twenty-one years more and never spoke to anyone. And if anyone would talk about God, he would weep tears of ecstasy. After that he wrote more books, including a commentary on the *Mahimnastotra—Hymns of the Lord.*

When we have gone through intellectual gymnastics, we find something beyond the intellect. A stage comes when intellect cannot guide us, and only intuition can show us the way. Intellect examines, calculates, decides, accepts, and rejects all that is happening within the spheres of mind, but intuition is an uninterrupted flow that dawns spontaneously from its source, deep down within. It dawns only when the mind attains a state of tranquility, equilibrium, and equanimity. That pure intuition expands the human consciousness in a way that one starts seeing things clearly. Life as a whole is understood, and ignorance is dispelled. After a series of experiences, direct experience becomes a guide and one starts receiving intuition spontaneously.

Suddenly a thought flashed in my mind, and I remembered the saying of the great sage Tulsidasa: "Without being God-fearing, love for God is not possible, and without love for God, realization is impossible." The fear of God makes one aware of God-consciousness, but fear of the world creates anxiety and thus danger. This atheistic swami became God-fearing when he experienced God-consciousness. Intellectual gymnastics is a mere exercise that creates fears, but love of God liberates one from all fears.

AN APPOINTMENT WITH DEATH

The first part of this story took place when I was seven years old, and its conclusion when I was twenty-eight.

When I was seven, several learned pandits and astrologers from Banaras were invited by one of my relatives to consider my future. India is famous for this science. You will find many charlatans, but you'll also find genuine astrological practitioners. If you decide to consult one, he may write a description of your whole life before you arrive. It will be waiting for you when you arrive, even if you have not told anyone you are going to see him. Such an ability is rare, but it is quite genuine.

I was standing just outside the door, listening to these astrologers. They all said, "This boy is going to die at the age of twenty-eight." They even gave the exact day.

I was so upset that I started sobbing. Then I thought, "I have such a short span of time. I will die without accomplishing anything. How am I possibly going to complete the mission of my life?"

My master came to me and inquired, "Why are you weeping?"

"I am going to die," I told him.

He asked, "And who told you that?"

I said, "All these people," and pointed to the astrologers gathered inside.

He took hold of my hand and said, "Come." He took me into the room and confronted the astrologers." Do you really mean to say that this lad is going to die at the age of twenty-eight?" he asked.

The unanimous response was "Yes."

"Are you sure?"

"Yes, he is going to die at that time, and nobody has the power to prevent it."

My master turned to me and said, "Do you know, these astrologers will all die before you do, and you will live for a long time because I will give you my own years." They said, "How is such a thing possible?"

My master replied, "Your prediction is wrong. There is something beyond astrology." Then he said to me, "Don't worry, but you will have to experience death face-to-face on that fateful day." Today none of those astrologers is alive. They all died before I was twenty-eight years old.

During the intervening years I forgot all about what had been predicted. When I was twenty-eight my master asked me to go to a mountain peak some eleven thousand feet high about sixty miles from Rishikesh. There I performed a ritual Durga Puja. I wore wooden sandals, a loincloth, and a shawl. I carried a pot of water with me, and nothing else. I went about freely in the mountains, chanting and reciting the hymns of the Divine Mother. The mountains were my home. I once climbed to a height of twenty thousand feet, and I was confident that I could climb any mountain without special equipment.

One day I was singing as I walked all alone beside a steep cliff, feeling like the Lord himself in that solitude. I was on my way to the top of the mountain, where there was a small temple, to worship the Divine Mother. There were pine trees all around. Suddenly I slipped on the pine needles and began to roll down the mountain. I thought that my life was finished, but as I plummeted down about five hundred feet, I was caught by a small, thorny bush. A sharp branch pierced me in the abdomen, and that held me. There was a precipitous drop below, and the bush started swinging with my weight. First I would see the mountains, and then the Ganga far below. I closed my eyes. When I opened them again, I saw blood flowing where the branch pierced my abdomen, but that was nothing compared to the stark imminence of death. I paid no attention to the pain because of the larger concern—the anticipation of death.

I repeated all the mantras I knew. I even repeated Christian and Buddhist mantras. I had been to many monasteries and had learned mantras from all faiths, but no mantra worked. I remembered many deities: I said, "O Bright Being such-and-such, please help me." But no help was forthcoming. There was only one thing that I had not tested—my courage! When I started testing my courage, I suddenly remembered, "I am not going to die, for there is no death for my soul. And death for this body is inevitable but unimportant. I am eternal. Why am I afraid? I have been identifying myself with my body. What a poor fool I have been!"

I remained suspended on that bush for about twenty minutes. Then I remembered something my master had told me. He said, "Do not form this habit, but whenever you really need me and remember me, I will be there, in one way or another."

I thought, "I have tested my courage; now I think I should also test my master." (This is natural for a disciple. He constantly wants to test his master. He avoids facing his own weaknesses by looking for faults in his master.) Because of the excessive bleeding I began to feel dizzy. Everything became hazy, and I began to lose consciousness.

Then I heard some women on the path just above me. They had come to the mountains to collect grass and roots for their animals. One of them looked down and saw me. She cried, "Look, a dead man!"

I thought, "If they think that I am dead, they will leave me like this." How could I communicate to them? My head was down and my feet were upward. They were a few hundred feet away. I couldn't speak, so I started waving my legs.

They said, "No, no, he's not dead—his legs are still moving. He must still be alive." They were brave women and came down, tied a rope around my waist, and lifted me up.

The stem was still inside me. I thought, "This is surely a time for courage." I pressed my stomach in and I pulled the stem out of my abdomen. They took me to a small mountain path. They asked me if I could walk, and I said, "Yes." At first I didn't realize the severity of my condition, for the injury caused by the stem was mostly internal. They thought that since I was a swami I could take care of myself without their help. They told me to follow the path until I came to a village; then they went on their way. I tried to walk, but after a few minutes I fainted and fell. I thought of my master and said to him, "My life is over. You brought me up and did everything for me. But now I am dying without realization."

Suddenly my master appeared. I thought my mind was playing tricks on me. I said, "Are you really here? I thought you had left me!" He said, "Why do you worry? Nothing is going to happen to you. Don't you remember that this is the time and date predicted for your death? You need face death no more today. You are all right now."

I gradually came to my senses. He brought some leaves, crushed them, and put them on the wound. He took me to a nearby cave and asked someone there to care for me. He said, "Even death can be prevented."

Then he went away. In two weeks the wound was healed, but the scar is still on my body.

In that experience I saw how a genuine and selfless master helps his disciple even if he is far away. I realized that the relationship between master and disciple is the highest and purest of all. It is indescribable.

chapter seven

Learning to Soar

Swami Rama's entire life was an adventure in faith. Trusting in a higher power—a power whose existence his spiritual mentors revealed to him again and again—he set out to change the world. With a handful of other yogis, he sparked the resurgence of interest in yoga in the West in the second half of the twentieth century. In India his philanthropic programs sent hundreds of students—who otherwise would never have been able to afford a higher education— on to school and successful careers. Thousands of lives have been saved at the hospital he single-handedly set out to build in order to serve the isolated villagers of the Himalayas. Faith, another great sage once said, can move mountains. Swami Rama moved many mountains.

But Swamiji would have been disgusted to hear me running on about his faith. For him what truly mattered was our response. Did we really hear what he's been trying to tell us—that there's far more to spiritual life than most of us ever imagined? And now that we know this, can we find the courage to embark on our own inner quest? Can we find the patience to persist in our prayers and yoga and meditation until the inner light begins to shine? Because if we do, it will.

Swami Rama left his body in November 1996. He was sitting with several of his students, told them he was going to depart, and left in full consciousness. Unlike many of us, he was not afraid to die because he knew where he was going. He had already explored the terrain ahead.

We can fly without wings if we launch, with full faith, into the sky of spirit. Great souls have gone on before us, showing us the way.

How can you launch your own voyage of the spirit? Drawing on the tradition of the Himalayan masters, Swami Rama offers some practical advice.

GRACE AND SELF-EFFORT

*B*elief in God and experiencing the presence of God at every moment are two different things. Before the actual, direct experience of the truth, you may believe in the existence of God, but your belief remains imperfect. True belief, which is known as faith, will come after you experience the truth directly. Faith born from direct experience becomes a part of your being. Like a compassionate mother, such faith protects you, guides you, and helps you remain unperturbed in all circumstances of life.

Self-realization is a matter of revelation that comes through God's grace. However, relying on God's grace and abandoning self-effort, especially in the early stage of *sadhana* [spiritual practice] is a big mistake. God's grace is like rain that falls over a vast area without any regard for the particular spots that it will benefit. It rains on the unjust and the just alike. And even after it rains, land that does not have good soil, or soil that cannot hold the waters, will remain barren. But when it rains on fertile land that has been properly prepared, seeds sprout and plants thrive. Only when we are fully prepared can we receive, assimilate, and benefit from divine grace.

Grace often dawns in the heart in a mysterious way. When it happens, we are awestruck; we are pulled into a state of wonder. Freedom from fear and doubt is the surest sign that we have received the grace of the Divine. Thereafter, worry and grief disappear forever. This is what the scriptures call "immortality." This immortality does not refer to the immortality of the body. It is the knowledge of the immortal self. After gaining this knowledge, fear associated with the decay, death, and destruction of the body vanishes. The person is free from fear of bondage and desire for liberation. Such a one is a *jivanmukta*—one who is liberated here and now.

When awakening comes, we can completely transform our personalities, throwing off the past. Some of the greatest sages in the world had been very bad—like Saul, who became Saint Paul. Suddenly, the day of awakening came for Saul on the road to Damascus, and his personality was transformed. Don't condemn yourself. No matter how bad or how small you think you have been, you have a chance to transform your whole personality. A true seeker can always realize the reality and attain freedom from all bondage and miseries. In just one second you can enlighten yourself.

The grace of God is pouring in, but you have a hole in your bowl. How can you retain God's grace? Sealing the hole caused by fear, doubt, hatred, anger, jealousy, greed, desire, and attachment is an integral part of spiritual practice. Once you make all sincere efforts and are truly exhausted, then you cry out in despair. That spontaneous cry is the highest form of prayer. It opens the channels of devotion, leading to a state of ecstasy. This state of ecstasy is called the grace of God. Grace is the fruit you receive from your faithful and sincere efforts.

The descent of divine grace is also known as *shaktipata*. Without purification and self-discipline we cannot receive, retain, and assimilate divine grace. When a student is ready, the master appears and confers the appropriate initiation. When a student has done his sadhana sincerely and faithfully, then the subtlest obstacle is removed by the divine grace that flows through the master. In other words, when you have done your duty gracefully you reap the fruit gracefully, too. That is shaktipata.

A genuine spiritual teacher, one who is assigned to teach according to tradition, searches out good students. He looks for certain signs and symptoms. He wants to know who is prepared. No student can fool a master. The master easily perceives who is prepared and who is not. If he finds the student is not yet ready, he will gradually prepare him for the higher teachings. When the wick and oil are properly prepared, the master lights the lamp. That is his role. The resulting light is divine.

THE JOURNEY INWARD

To practice meditation, first you must have a strong, burning desire. Such a strong desire leads to commitment. Commitment needs to be nourished by the power of determination. When you are determined that today you will sit in meditation, no one has the power to disturb you.

A firm conviction is essential for establishing a definite philosophy of life. Intellect intervenes, and blind emotion misguides. Though both are great powers, they should be known first, analyzed, and then directed toward the source of intuition. Intuition is the only source of true knowledge. Every human being is fully equipped to open the channel of intuition. A disciplined mind, proper guidance, and regular practice are the keys.

Do not expect too much in the beginning. There is no instant method of meditation. Expectation will force you to fantasize, imagine, and hallucinate. Expectation will lead you to anxiety, and anxiety will not allow you to meditate. As a result you will be frustrated and you will stop meditating.

As far as technique is concerned, first relax your body and mind. Calm your breath. Detach yourself from the external world and watch your breath. It is the most tangible manifestation of the Divine.

As part of a systematic method of meditation, first learn to sit with your head, neck, and trunk straight. It is the healthiest and most comfortable way of sitting. The pressure at the base of the spine creates heat, and as heat increases, the pranic force expands and rises upward. Because the spine is straight and the nervous system is relaxed, the pranic energy flows freely upward along the spinal column toward the head. In this pose you are free from sloth and inertia. Without the proper posture you will face numberless obstacles in your meditation.

For any practice you need a strong, healthy body. When you practice regularly in one sitting posture for a long time, your body will become still, the breath serene, and the mind tranquil. Then you will realize that you are not the body—you have a body. You will also understand that the body is a wonderful instrument and you should take care of it properly. An unhealthy body dissipates the mind—you will have no time to work with other aspects of yourself. That is why maintaining physical health is an integral part of spiritual practice.

FULFILLING YOUR RESPONSIBILITIES

Regardless of your profession, you can attain the highest goal of your life by performing your actions selflessly, lovingly, and skillfully. This is called Karma Yoga. If you are a doctor, transform your medical practice into worship. Treat your patients selflessly and lovingly. Consider the money you get from your practice to be the gift of providence. Remember that you are an instrument in the hands of the Divine. It is a privilege that the Divine has chosen you for this job. It is the Divine within you serving the Divine that dwells in the patients.

This awareness will infuse your action with a spiritual consciousness. Your simple actions will thus turn into Karma Yoga—a sublime spiritual practice. It will prevent you from being bound by the rope of success and failure. The awareness that the Divine within is using you as an instrument will help you disidentify yourself from your action as well as its fruit. It will help you remain free from egoism. You will become the best doctor, for example, and yet you will remain free from the identification of being the best doctor. By performing your duties in such a manner, all your negative karmas will be destroyed. The fruits of your virtuous deeds will mature into *bhakti,* the unwavering love and devotion for the Divine Being. Your heart will be filled with the nectar of immortal love. Inebriated with that love, you will not have any desires—not even the desire for liberation.

The stream of life is eternal. This present life is a continuation of the previous life. The subtle force of life is beyond birth and death. To reap our karmic fruits, we are born; and when our karmas are exhausted, we leave this place. Karmas remaining from the past and the new karmas we create in this lifetime force us to come back again. The seed of karma was planted long ago. The karmic fruits we are reaping in the present are linked to our previous life. There is no way we can attain freedom without discharging our karmas. Therefore, we must learn to perform our duties lovingly and selflessly. That is the way to freedom.

Childhood is the foundation for the whole life. Ideas instilled in childhood last forever. The education imparted in early childhood has a greater influence on us than the education received in the universities. A child should be taught self-reliance, self-trust, and self-confidence. Childhood is the age of faith. If you tell children they are dull-witted, they become timid and lose confidence in themselves. The parents' role in a child's growth is of the utmost importance. The mother is the first teacher, then the father, and then the teachers in the school.

Unconditional love is the ground for raising a child. Do not impose your values on them, either. Don't force them to refrain from doing what you do yourself. Children learn from example, not from commandments. To discipline and educate properly, first you have to discipline and educate yourself.

Parents ruin their children's lives when they try to fulfill their desires and ambitions through their children. Such children may not express their resentment when they are young, but once they are grown their hatred will manifest. Such ignorant parents put the blame on "modern education." However, if you raise your child with love and sincerity, it will give you an opportunity to see what your strengths and weaknesses are. If you raise your child selflessly, lovingly, and skillfully, by the time the child has grown, you will have become wise.

TASTING BEAUTY AND JOY

Searching for peace and happiness, the mind runs from one object to another. Once it gets a taste of inner happiness it will not be distracted by the charms and temptations of the world. An outwardly oriented mind expects long-lasting joy from short-lived objects. Upon not finding that permanent joy in short-lived objects, it blames God, providence, or the external world. The enlightened part of ourselves tells us that the Divine Being within is the center of perfect happiness, but, lacking inner awareness, the mind refuses to believe the Divine within and receive guidance from it.

Happiness is your own creation. If you expect something or someone to make you happy, then forget it. Achieving the objects of your desire will not make you happy. It may give you a momentary thrill or feeling of security, but you will soon be engulfed by fear of loss. Happiness is a condition of mind that is created by your conviction that nothing in this world is worth enough to worry about. The more you maintain this conviction, the stronger the habit of happiness you form. This habit then becomes an integral part of your being.

You have everything you need to be happy. You have a beautiful body equipped with fully developed limbs, organs, and senses. Your intelligence supersedes the intelligence of all other creatures. Nature has given you the privilege of modifying and reconstructing your surroundings, both externally and internally. You can accomplish anything you want, provided you have confidence in your self-effort and in God's grace.

Simple living and elevated thought help in creating an aesthetic sense. It takes a long time to create this aesthetic sense and to incorporate grace and beauty into our lives. Costly dresses have no power to hide our ugliness; stylish clothes do not have the power to make us beautiful. Instead of focusing on externals, we should learn to cultivate and express our inner beauty.

THE HIGHEST PATH

*B*eginners often argue and boast about the superiority of their way, but one who has trodden the path knows that all paths lead to the same destination. There is no superior or inferior path. It is immaterial which path one follows, but one should carefully watch the modifications of one's own mind and learn not to identify with them.

All the great religions have come out of one truth. Experiential knowledge is the foundation of all religions. The founders of all religions were practitioners of meditation. They taught only what they practiced. They had one common characteristic: love. Their love was not confined to a particular community. By loving all, they worshiped God, for they knew that one single truth has manifested in all living beings. This experience motivated them to teach the gospel of love. Thus, love is the heart of religion. Religion plays an important role in bringing people together, by teaching them to love all and exclude none.

People accept religious leaders as authorities. We must not forget, however, that any religious or spiritual teacher is simply a channel for the ancient wisdom. Leader worship is the ground for the creation of a cult. The tradition of the sages does not allow hero worship. The essence of the practice in this tradition lies in loving all and keeping the mind focused on the Divine within. Religion without love is lifeless. To practice love you must not hate anyone, especially those who do not belong to your religion, culture, or community.

THE SECRET OF THE UNIVERSE

*W*hy are the sun, moon, and stars constantly on the move? If you know the purpose of their movement, then move in harmony with them. If you do not know, move in harmony with them still, for by doing so, one day you will know the purpose.

Here, there, everywhere, there is only one Divine Force. She pervades and permeates everything. Seated in the lotus of the heart, she animates all living beings. I pray to that light, the Mistress of Life.

There is only one mother—the Divine Mother. She is of unsurpassed beauty and bliss. We, her children, have inherited this same beauty and bliss. All of the actions we perform throughout our lives are divine sports played in her courtyard. Ignorance of this truth is bondage. To know it is liberation.

The creator knows why She created the world. Through your thought, speech, and action, add to the beauty and bliss in the world. That is called "worship." Worship nature and her children, and nature will adore you.

"Keep walking, keep walking," say the sages. Your heart and lungs never stop working. Once they do stop, you are no longer alive. Be creative and productive. The greatest sin you can commit is to be lazy and slothful.

All I have is the gift of love, which I received from my master and other sages. This same gift I offer to you. May you receive, retain, and multiply it in your heart. God bless you.

ABOUT THE AUTHOR

One of the greatest adepts, teachers, writers, and humanitarians of the twentieth century, Swami Rama is the founder of the Himalayan Institute. Born in northern India, he was raised from early childhood by a Himalayan sage, Bengali Baba. Under the guidance of his master he traveled from monastery to monastery and studied with a variety of Himalayan saints and sages, including his grand-master, who was living in a remote region of Tibet. In addition to this intense spiritual training, Swami Rama received higher education in both India and Europe. From 1949 to 1952, he held the prestigious position of Shankaracharya of Karvirpitham in south India. Thereafter, he returned to his master to receive further training at his cave monastery, and in 1969 came to the United States where he founded the Himalayan Institute. His best-known work, *Living with the Himalayan Masters,* reveals the many facets of this exceptional adept and demonstrates his embodiment of the living tradition of the East.

THE HIMALAYAN INSTITUTE

The main building of the Institute headquarters near Honesdale, Pennsylvania

Founded in 1971 by Swami Rama, the Himalayan Institute has been dedicated to helping people grow physically, mentally, and spiritually by combining the best knowledge of both the East and the West.

Our international headquarters is located on a beautiful 400-acre campus in the rolling hills of the Pocono Mountains of northeastern Pennsylvania. The atmosphere here is one to foster growth, increase inner awareness, and promote calm. Our grounds provide a wonderfully peaceful and healthy setting for our seminars and extended programs. Students from all over the world join us here to attend programs in such diverse areas as hatha yoga, meditation, stress reduction, ayurveda, nutrition, Eastern philosophy, psychology, and other subjects. Whether the programs are for weekend meditation retreats, week-long seminars on spirituality, months-long residential programs, or holistic health services, the attempt here is to provide an environment of gentle inner progress. We invite you to join with us in the ongoing process of personal growth and development.

The Institute is a nonprofit organization. Your membership in the Institute helps to support its programs. Please call or write for information on becoming a member.

PROGRAMS AND SERVICES INCLUDE:
- Weekend or extended seminars and workshops
- Meditation retreats and advanced meditation instruction
- Hatha yoga teachers' training
- Residential programs for self-development
- Holistic health services and pancha karma at the Institute's Center for Health and Healing
- Spiritual excursions
- Varcho Veda® herbal products
- Himalayan Institute Press®
- *Yoga International* magazine
- Sanskrit correspondence course

A Quarterly Guide to Programs and Other Offerings is free within the United States. To request a copy, or for further information, call 800-822-4547 or 570-253-5551; write to the Himalayan Institute, 952 Bethany Turnpike, Building 1, Honesdale, PA 18431, USA; or visit our Web site at www.HimalayanInstitute.org.

HIMALAYAN INSTITUTE®
P R E S S

The Himalayan Institute Press has long been regarded as "The Resource for Holistic Living." We publish dozens of titles, as well as audio and video-tapes that offer practical methods for living harmoniously and achieving inner balance. Our approach addresses the whole person—body, mind, and spirit—integrating the latest scientific knowledge with ancient healing and self-development techniques.

As such, we offer a wide array of titles on physical and psychological health and well-being, spiritual growth through meditation and other yogic practices, as well as translations of yogic scriptures.

Our yoga accessories include the Japa Kit for meditation practice and the Neti Pot™, the ideal tool for sinus and allergy sufferers. Our Varcho Veda® line of quality herbal extracts is now available to enhance balanced health and well-being.

Subscriptions are available to a bimonthly magazine, *Yoga International,* which offers thought-provoking articles on all aspects of meditation and yoga, including yoga's sister science, ayurveda.

For a free catalog, call 800-822-4547 or 570-253-5551; e-mail hibooks@HimalayanInstitute.org; fax 570-647-1552; write to the Himalayan Institute Press, 630 Main St., Suite 350, Honesdale, PA 18431-1843, USA; or visit our Web site at www.HimalayanInstitute.org.

discover
more of
yourself

Happiness Is Your Creation
Swami Rama as compiled by Pandit Rajmani Tigunait, Ph.D.

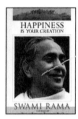

"You are a creation of God, but happiness is your creation. You are equipped with everything that you need to live a happy life. Your only job is to discover the source of happiness within and infuse your surroundings with that inner happiness."

—SWAMI RAMA

In *Happiness Is Your Creation*, Pandit Tigunait gathered the inspirational teachings of his master, Swami Rama. Yoga is the path of self-discipline, self-mastery, and self-realization. Learn where you come from, what the purpose of your life is, and how to live a joyful, productive, and peaceful life. The passages in this enriching book identify the causes of unhappiness and provide direction to keep centered and joyful.

Paperback with flaps / 5 ½ x 8 ½ / 136 pages / $12.95
ISBN 0-89389-246-7

Touched by Fire
The Ongoing Journey of a Spiritual Seeker
Pandit Rajmani Tigunait, Ph.D.

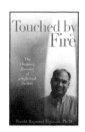

This is the autobiography of a remarkable spiritual leader who shares his travels, experiences, and encounters with numerous teachers, sages, and his mentor, Swami Rama of the Himalayas. Follow Pandit Tigunait's life as it began in a small town in India that hasn't changed in over 1,000 years, to his current standing as spiritual head of the Himalayan Institute. His journey is filled with years of disciplined study and the struggle to master the lessons and skills passed to him. This book brings Western society a glimpse of Eastern philosophies in a clear, understandable fashion. *Touched by Fire* goes further to dispel the many misconceptions surrounding yoga and meditation.

Paperback with flaps / 5 ½ x 8 ½ / 296 pages / $16.95
ISBN 0-89389-239-4

050733